C Is for
Christmas

An A to Z Guide

Is for Christmas

The History, Personalities, and Meaning of Christ's Birth

David W. Wiersbe and Warren W. Wiersbe

BakerBooks

a division of Baker Publishing Group
Grand Rapids, Michigan

© 2012 by ScripTex Inc.

Published by Baker Books
a division of Baker Publishing Group
P.O. Box 6287, Grand Rapids, MI 49516-6287
www.bakerbooks.com

Printed in the United States of America

Library of Congress Cataloging-in-Publication Data
Wiersbe, David.
    C is for Christmas : the history, personalities, and meaning of Christ's birth
/ David W. Wiersbe and Warren W. Wiersbe.
        p.   cm.
    ISBN 978-0-8010-1489-5 (pbk.)
    1. Jesus Christ—Nativity—Dictionaries. 2. Christmas—Dictionaries. I.
Wiersbe, Warren W. II. Title
BT315.3.W54 2012
232.92—dc23   2012012149

12   13   14   15   16   17   18   7   6   5   4   3   2   1

Contents

– Contents –

Preface

Throughout the centuries, so many traditions have woven themselves into Christmas that it's becoming difficult to understand what the Advent season is all about. This book is an attempt to add some depth of meaning and some spiritual insight to your Christmas celebration. We don't want you celebrating Christmas wearing a blindfold.

The better we understand the historical and doctrinal foundations of the magnificent Christmas event, the more exciting and enriching this special day becomes. Christmas is about the greatest of miracles—the Lord coming to earth as a human being—and it offers to the world the greatest of gifts—eternal life. "For God did not send his Son into the world to condemn the world, but to save the world through him" (John 3:17).

We suggest you have a Bible at hand as you read. To get the most out of this book, you should look up the biblical references and ponder them.

> O come let us adore Him,
> Christ the Lord!

David W. Wiersbe
Warren W. Wiersbe

ADVENT

The word *advent* means "coming" and refers to Jesus Christ's coming to earth as an infant and to His promised return to earth known as the "second coming."

Right after Thanksgiving, two grandsons called their grandmother to announce that they had begun decorating the house for Christmas. "And guess what? We got to set up our baby Jesus action figures!" For most of us, the nativity scene is the most common mental picture of Advent. But Advent is far more than the baby in the manger, as you will discover.

Advent, Christ's First

KNOWING THE MESSIAH

The first question to ask about Christ's first coming is, *How would the world know the Messiah?*

Christ's first advent fulfills a long progression of specific prophecies. God Himself, in Genesis 3:15, predicted that a human descendant of Adam and Eve would crush Satan's head. Israel came to expect that the Messiah would be like Moses, based on

Deuteronomy 18:18: "I will raise up a prophet from among their countrymen like you, and I will put My words in his mouth, and he shall speak to them all that I command him" (NASB).

God's covenant with Abraham meant that his offspring, the nation of Israel, had a special relationship to God, and through Abraham's line all the families of the earth would be blessed (Gen. 12:1–3). The patriarch Jacob foretold that the Messiah would come from the tribe of Judah (49:10). God's promise to David was that one day one of David's descendants would reign on his throne forever (see 2 Sam. 7:12–16). Isaiah predicted that Messiah would be born of a virgin (Isa. 7:14). Bethlehem was to be the site of Messiah's birth (Mic. 5:2).

Putting the prophecies together, Messiah would be a human being, a Jew from the tribe of Judah, in the line of King David, born of a virgin in the town of Bethlehem. By fulfilling these prophecies, Jesus Christ confirms that He alone is the One sent from God to be our Savior.

CHRIST'S HUMAN NATURE

Another question about Christ's first coming that requires an answer is, *Why did God take on a human nature and body?*

The New Testament affirms consistently that God the Son took on a human body and nature, so that Jesus is uniquely fully God and fully human. "The Word became flesh" (John 1:14), and the word for "flesh" means skin and bone and blood. John contends that only those who confess that Jesus Christ came "in the flesh" belong to God (1 John 4:2). Paul refers to Jesus in an early confession of faith as "He who was revealed in the flesh" (1 Tim. 3:16). The writer to the Hebrews agrees: "Since the children share in flesh and blood, He Himself likewise also partook of the same" (Heb. 2:14 NASB). God's holiness requires that sin be judged, and the wages of sin is death (Rom. 6:23). Because of Adam and Eve's sin, every human being has entered the world with an inner bent toward sin (5:12). Sin is inbred, not only a learned behavior. To redeem sinful human beings, the Redeemer must be a human being (Heb. 2:14–15; Gal. 4:4–5).

But the Redeemer must be sinless; that is, He must have no sins of His own for which to pay. John the Baptist identified Jesus as "the Lamb of God, who takes away the sin of the world" (John 1:29). "Lamb" refers to a Passover lamb, which had to be perfect in every way. The implication is that Jesus was perfect and therefore could be the substitute sacrificed for humanity's sin. (For other affirmations of Christ's sinlessness, see John 8:46; 2 Cor. 5:21; Heb. 4:15; 1 Peter 2:22; 1 John 3:5.)

To bring salvation, the Redeemer must right what our first parents did wrong. Jesus is referred to as the Second Adam because He restored what Adam had lost (see 1 Cor. 15:45). "God made Him who knew no sin to be sin on our behalf, that we might become the righteousness of God in Him" (2 Cor. 5:21 NASB). "For as through the one man's disobedience the many were made sinners, even so through the obedience of the One the many will be made righteous" (Rom. 5:19 NASB). Charles Wesley put it this way: "Second Adam from above, reinstate us in Thy love."

The Son of God became fully human to identify with sinful humans, to live a sinless life, to sacrifice Himself in our place to atone for our sin, and to rise again to conquer death and give believing sinners the gift of eternal life. Jesus volunteered for this mission and willingly endured the suffering to bring glory to His Father, to receive a name above every name, and to transform sinners into saints who glorify God.

We should worship the Lord Jesus for leaving heaven's glories, for condescending to become human, and for voluntarily embracing the limitations of a human body. Because Jesus did this, we know that He understands what bodily existence is like for us. We can also look forward to having a body like His resurrection body!

THE PURPOSE OF HIS COMING

One further question about Christ's first advent needs a response: *What did Jesus come to earth to do?* To answer this question briefly, we turn to several texts in 1 John where the author uses the words "appeared" or "manifested" to address the reasons for the incarnation.

Sin is humanity's biggest problem, and Jesus came to solve that problem. "You know that He appeared in order to take away sins; and in Him there is no sin" (1 John 3:5 NASB). God takes sin seriously, and so should we. In "appearing," God identified with sinners. He "became flesh" (John 1:14). In His life Jesus modeled perfect obedience to God, and in His death He atoned for humankind's sin. The result of Christ's life, death, and resurrection is that God makes sinners holy when they trust Jesus Christ as their Savior.

Jesus' arrival on planet Earth was a declaration of war on Satan. "The Son of God appeared for this purpose, to destroy the works of the devil" (1 John 3:8 NASB). This verse emphasizes the reality of Satan and his opposition to God and God's people. We must not underestimate the hostility and deceitfulness of the enemy of our souls. Jesus certainly did not. The word "destroy" in 1 John 3:8 points to the power of God's Son. To "destroy" means to dissolve the bonds that hold things together. Rather than an all-out frontal assault, Jesus quietly undid Satan's strategy by obeying Scripture, depending on the Holy Spirit, and loving His Father. Satan thought the cross was the end of Jesus; instead, it was the downfall of Satan's plan. Satan is still active today, but his defeat is certain (see Revelation 20).

Christ's coming to earth was an expression of God's love. How do we know that God loves sinners? "By this the love of God was manifested in us, that God has sent His only begotten Son into the world so that we might live through Him. In this is love, not that we loved God, but that He loved us and sent His Son to be the propitiation for our sins" (1 John 4:9–10 NASB). These verses provide three evidences that God truly loves us:

1. God initiated the relationship (He sent His Son).
2. God gave His best (His only begotten Son).
3. God met our deepest needs. (We can live through Him, who is the propitiation for our sins. *Propitiation* means satisfying God's holy wrath against sin.)

When we don't feel that God loves us, we need to look at objective truth. God reached out to us by sending the Son He loves, and the Son died for our sins and rose to give us an eternal relationship with God. Is Jesus *your* Savior?

Advent, Christ's Second

Jesus promised that He would come back: "I will come again and receive you to Myself, that where I am, there you may be also" (John 14:3 NASB). The Revelation of St. John ends with the Lord's declaration, "I am coming quickly" (Rev. 22:20 NASB). Since He ascended into heaven, Jesus' disciples have been looking for His return. There are differences in how Christians interpret the time and order of Christ's return, but there is universal agreement that He will come again. This belief is what orients the season of Advent toward the future.

Christ's Second Advent is a motive for keeping ourselves pure. "We know that when He appears, we will be like Him, because we will see Him just as He is. And everyone who has this hope fixed on Him purifies himself" (1 John 3:2–3 NASB). Because we do not know the time of His return and because we want to meet Him unashamed, we must not let sin master us.

For us, the Second Advent will mean a release from bodily limitations. When Christ comes from heaven, He "will transform the body of our humble state into conformity with the body of His glory" (Phil. 3:21 NASB). Our bodies are a spiritual battle-ground, and disease and time take their physical toll. Christ's return means having a body like that of our risen Lord.

The Second Advent spells the final defeat of Satan (Revelation 19–20). The war that has been waged since the Garden of Eden will finally come to an end. Resistance to Christ the King will cease as Satan and all his followers are judged and sent to their eternal punishment.

Christ's return will usher in the new heaven and earth (Revelation 21–22). The description of the eternal state begins by naming what will *not* be there: no tears, no death, no mourning, no crying, no pain (21:4), no night (v. 25), and no curse (22:3). Wounds will be healed (v. 4), there will be peace, and we will see our Savior face-to-face. "And so shall we ever be with the Lord" (1 Thess. 4:17 KJV).

The return of the King is anticipated only by those who believe in Him. Ultimately, every knee will bow and every tongue will confess that Jesus Christ is Lord (Phil. 2:10–11). The choice is to submit to Him now, voluntarily, or refuse and be forced to acknowledge His lordship when He comes to reign.

Advent, the Season

The Church year begins with the season of Advent, and as we've seen, this is a time when Christians look back to Christ's first coming in Bethlehem and look ahead to His coming again.

Our readers may question this emphasis on Advent. After all, there's nothing in Scripture that commands Christians to keep this season. Some churches do not keep seasons and emphasize only Good Friday and Easter. We are certainly not insisting that every believer must acknowledge Advent, nor should it be a test of Christian fellowship. Just as Americans recognize the Fourth of July and Thanksgiving Day, Christians mark important events in the life of the Church.

Consider that one of God's gifts to Israel was a calendar. As Israel prepared to exit Egypt, God told Moses that Passover was to be celebrated on the fourteenth day of the first month in the Jewish year (Exod. 12:1–6, 14). From this decree, the rest of the Jewish feasts and fasts and holy days followed in an annual cycle (see Leviticus 23). Since God established for Israel events and experiences to be repeated and commemorated, it is reasonable to embrace a calendar for the Christian Church.

The Christian year has been designed around the key events in the life of the Lord Jesus and the life of the Church. It begins with the seasons of Advent and Epiphany and then moves to Ordinary Time. The season of Lent precedes the Church's commemoration of the triumphal entry and the death and resurrection of our Lord. Ascension is forty days after the Festival of the Resurrection, followed by the season of Pentecost (with its emphasis on Christlikeness). The final Sunday in the year is known as Christ the King, completing the annual cycle. These events provide a range of themes with which to shape worship services and sermons. Incorporating the events of Christ's life into our calendar has a way of sanctifying time and of putting our lives in rhythm with God's saving work.

The season of Advent begins on the Sunday closest to November 30. It includes the four Sundays prior to Christmas and concludes on Christmas Eve.

The season of Advent was first mentioned in writing about AD 380 in Spain, as a time of fasting prior to celebrating the nativity. Not until the fourth century was the date for Christmas settled, and it is still a point of difference between Western and Eastern churches. By the sixth century, monks in Tours, France, were keeping a pre-Christmas fast, and by 581 most churches made pre-Christmas preparations. By the end of the century, the four Sundays before Christmas were known as Advent Sundays.

SEASON OF PENITENCE

The season of Advent embraces several "moods." It is *a time of preparation*, not only for a holiday, but to ready our hearts, minds, and lives to celebrate God's gift of salvation in Christ. It is also *a season of penitence*, which we do in preparation for meeting our Savior. God's people are to confess sin, repent of it, and walk on the highway of holiness (Isaiah 35). Scriptures from the Psalms and Prophets, chosen for this season, encourage a feeling of dissatisfaction with the way things are and a deep desire for God to bring change.

SEASON OF HOPE

Advent is *a season of waiting in hope*. Israel's prophets pointed to the coming Messiah, but it was centuries before the time was right for God to send His Son (Gal. 4:4). The people of Israel longed for their deliverer to come, and this longing

C Is for Christmas

created a sense of expectancy. The Advent hymns "Come, Thou Long-Expected Jesus" and "O Come, O Come, Emmanuel" beautifully express this hope.

Today children can hardly wait until they can open their presents, and the waiting seems like a punishment. Advent is an opportunity to be productive while learning patience. Not only do we "wait for" Christ to come or for Christmas Eve to arrive, we also "wait with" each other and pursue activities that redeem the time. Often Advent worship services end with the words, "Come quickly, Lord Jesus!" (see Rev. 22:20).

SEASON OF REFLECTION

Advent is *a season of reflection*, when we meditate on the events of Christ's birth and the experiences of the many persons in the story and on the mystery of God taking on flesh. On a personal level, Advent encourages us to remember God's goodness to us and ponder how we can more intentionally honor Christ in our lives. Increasingly, Christians intentionally resist the cultural emphasis on money, buying, and giving. Attending only those events we want to experience creates a margin of time during a very busy time of year. Simplifying gift giving can make the gifts more meaningful (for instance, exchange with family members books you have enjoyed reading). Because Jesus was poor, it is right that we help those in need, and not just during Advent.

SEASON OF JOY

Advent should be *a season of joy*, although the unrestrained celebration of Christ's birth should wait for Christmas Day (for the purists). Many elements can contribute to a joyful spirit. Listening to a wide range of seasonal music will prevent your ears from being dulled by the music in the malls. Making gifts and preparing foods for the holiday increase our anticipation. Decorating the house (inside and out) affords another kind of enjoyment. Above all, joy should come from the true story of the joyful God bringing salvation to sinners so they could become His children.

- A -

Because Advent occurs when daylight is minimal, it is *a season of light*. For many congregations and families, a traditional, lighted Advent wreath or Advent log adds to the atmosphere of celebration. Lighting the candles symbolizes the growing brightness of Jesus, the Light of the world (John 8:12; 9:5). Many congregations do a candlelighting service on Christmas Eve, pointing to the Light that shines in the darkness, which the darkness can never extinguish (John 1:5).

The season of Advent concludes on Christmas Eve. Our celebration of Christ's birth does not end our looking for His return. In a spiritual sense, for Christ's followers, it is always the season of Advent because we constantly expect Him to return. At His incarnation, the eternal Lord entered time. Now we wait for time to end to enter eternity with our Lord.

The season of Advent will be as meaningful as you make it.

𝑒 See: Patience, Pondering

ANGELS

Angels are real. God created them to serve and praise Him (Heb. 1:7, 14; Isa. 6:2–3). They are spiritual beings who assume a human form when they appear. God created angels as a company, so their number is fixed, and they do not reproduce. Fallen angels cannot be saved, because Jesus died and rose only for sinful human beings. Angels "render service for the sake of those who will inherit salvation" (Heb. 1:14 NASB), and that service extends to little children (see Matt. 18:10).

Angelic Activity

The events surrounding Christ's birth are remarkable for the comings and goings of angels. First, the angel Gabriel announced to Zechariah that he and Elizabeth would have a child in their old age and that the child would be the forerunner of the Messiah (Luke 1:5–25). Zechariah found this hard to believe and his doubt resulted in his living the discipline of silence for nine months.

Next, Gabriel came to the Virgin Mary with the news that she was the chosen one to bear God's Son, David's heir, a holy Child (vv. 26–38). Mary questioned how this would happen, knowing she was a virgin. The question came from faith and not from doubt, and Gabriel's response pointed to the overshadowing work of God the Holy Spirit. Mary submitted to God's will and became pregnant.

Joseph, Mary's fiancé, was torn by the news of her pregnancy. He loved Mary, but if she had been unfaithful, he wanted a quiet divorce (in their culture engagement brought all the obligations of marriage with none of the benefits). An angel appeared to Joseph in a dream, confirming the manner in which Mary had become pregnant and affirming the identity and gender of her Child (Matt. 1:18–25). The angel also directed that two names be given to this Child: Jesus ("Jehovah saves" or "God is salvation") and Immanuel ("God is with us"). Joseph married Mary.

After Mary gave birth to baby Jesus in Bethlehem, an angel of the Lord appeared to shepherds in the fields outside the town. The blazing light of his arrival frightened the shepherds, and the good news he gave them about the birth of the Savior amazed them. This is the only time that angels proclaim the gospel. The angel gave a sign by which to find the newborn (Luke 2:12). Then a multitude of angels—a heavenly host—appeared to declare glory to God and peace on earth (vv. 13–14). (This has come down to us as the song of the angels, although the text says the angels were "saying" their piece. Still, might not angelic voices have a musical quality?)

Some time later, following the visit of the Magi, an angel of the Lord appeared again in Joseph's dream, telling him to take his family to Egypt to escape Herod's paranoid violence (Matt. 2:13). Joseph obeyed the traveling orders. After Herod died, an angel of the Lord appeared yet again in a dream to tell Joseph to take his family home (vv. 19–20).

The Meaning of the Angelic Activity

What are we to make of all this angelic activity?

First, the news brought by the angels could not have come from a human source. Zechariah and Elizabeth knew they were too old to become parents. Mary had kept herself pure and knew that pregnancy was not possible through human means. Joseph needed divine wisdom and guidance in his relationship with Mary and in caring for the infant Jesus. Thus in each case the word had to come from a supernatural source.

Next, the Son of God was coming to earth—a King entering His domain! In heaven, angels do God's bidding and offer ceaseless worship. How appropriate that heavenly servants be given a part in preparing the way for the Savior's birth! The paradox of the eternal Son of God entering time as a human must have astounded the angels. God's plan of salvation fulfilled by our Lord Jesus is something "into which angels long to look" (1 Pet. 1:12 NASB).

Further, each message from the angels focused on the person of Jesus, God's Son. Zechariah and Elizabeth's son, John the Baptist, was to prepare the way for Jesus' ministry. Mary was favored by God to carry the Son of God in her womb, providing His human nature and body. Joseph's angelic encounters spurred him to take Mary as his wife and to provide for and protect Mary and Jesus. The shepherds were directed to find the newborn Savior for themselves. The goal of each angelic encounter was pointing people to Jesus.

Finally, Jesus is superior to the angels (Heb. 1:4). He is superior to angels because He is the *Creator* (vv. 2–3), *God* (v. 3a, "exact representation"), the *Savior* (v. 3b; 2:16), and *King* (1:3, 8). Because of the exalted position of the Lord Jesus Christ, the worship of angels is wrong (see Col. 2:18).

God appoints His angels to serve and protect His people (Heb. 1:14). Angels are not a source of power for humans or a means of controlling circumstances, persons, or things. We are not to worship angels (Rev. 22:8–9). We do not pray to angels because they are not our intercessors ("For there is one God, and one mediator also between God and men, the man Christ Jesus"—1 Tim. 2:5 NASB). Angels worship and obey Jesus (Heb. 1:6–7). Jesus did not come to earth to save angels but to save "Abraham's descendants" (2:16). The apostle Paul stated that believers in Jesus will judge angels (1 Cor. 6:3). This truth implies, then, that the least of the redeemed human saints has a higher place with God than any angel!

Human beings continue to encounter angels because angels continue to be God's ministers to the saints on earth (Heb. 1:14). At times, when showing hospitality to strangers, God's people have entertained angels without knowing it (Genesis 18; Heb. 13:2). If you believe you have encountered an angel, evaluate the experience with these questions:

1. Whom do you praise, the angel or Christ who sent the angel?
2. Has the experience deepened your faith in Jesus Christ?
3. Are you looking for angels or looking at Jesus?

An eternal relationship with the living Savior is much better than an encounter with angels.

❧ See: Joseph, Light, Mary, Shepherds, Songs

ANNA

Many of the Jewish people who frequented the temple in the days of Caesar Augustus recognized Anna, an elderly widow, because she came to worship there each day. Some of them knew her personally; they had talked with her about her favorite subject—the coming of the promised Messiah (Luke 2:36–38).

She was too poor to own any scrolls of the prophets, but during her long life, she had often heard these promises read in the synagogue, and they were written permanently on her heart.

- A -

Perhaps her favorite was from the prophet Malachi—"'Then suddenly the Lord you are seeking will come to his temple; the messenger of the covenant, whom you desire, will come,' says the LORD Almighty" (Mal. 3:1).

And He did come!

As Anna entered the Court of the Women, she saw her friend Simeon standing by a couple with a baby, and Simeon was loudly praising the Lord. "Sovereign Lord, as you have promised, you may now dismiss your servant in peace. For my eyes have seen your salvation, which you have prepared in the sight of all nations: a light for revelation to the Gentiles, and the glory of your people Israel" (Luke 2:29–32). Anna joined the praise service and gave thanks to God that the Messiah had been born; then she went and spread the good news among her friends. She is still spreading that good news.

Anna could have given many excellent reasons for staying home from the temple—if nothing else, her age. Bible students interpret the data differently. Some say she was eighty-four years old at that time, while others say she had been a widow for eighty-four years. If she was married in her early teens, which was not unusual for Jewish girls, then she was twenty or twenty-one when her husband died; and if she had been a widow for eighty-four years, she would have been at least 104 or 105 years old at that time. The text says that she was "very old," and eighty-four could hardly be called "very old" even in that day. But whatever her age, she didn't allow it to keep her from the house of God. Like King David, she said, "One thing I ask from the LORD, this only do I seek: that I may dwell in the house of the LORD all the days of my life" (Ps. 27:4).

Keep in mind that widows in that day received no government assistance, as elderly people do today. Moses in the Law warned the Israelites not to neglect the widows and orphans, because they were beloved of God (Exodus 22–24; Deut. 14:28–29; Isa. 1:17). Each synagogue congregation sought to care for its own needy members, but congregations were not especially wealthy and the needs were many. There were other widows besides Anna.

We are not told that she had any physical afflictions, but surely she suffered from the normal ailments that attack older people. Moses died in perfect health (Deut. 34:5–7), but he was an exception. Anna and the rest of us must endure what Solomon described in Ecclesiastes 12. But if she had arthritic joints, poor hearing and vision, and general debilitation, her problems didn't keep her from being in God's house to worship, pray, and witness. These are excuses we use today but they would never have come to her mind.

She might have complained about the management of the temple and refused to worship there. Even Jesus called it "a den of robbers" and threw out the merchants and moneychangers (Luke 19:45–47). Surely she knew that the religious leaders of the nation were hirelings and not shepherds and had little concern for the needs of the people. But this didn't deter her from being in the temple day after day, worshiping God, and ministering to the people. She was a prophetess and some of the people looked to her for spiritual guidance.

No doubt, since her childhood, she had known the messianic promises that God had given to Israel and she believed they would be fulfilled. How long she had to wait! However, she never gave up but each day ministered in the temple where she hoped to meet the promised Messiah that Malachi wrote about. The Lord made sure that her timing was perfect on that one special day, and she was there just as Mary and Joseph had completed their sacrifices. The same Holy Spirit who led Anna brought Simeon to the temple too (2:27). As busy religious people walked past them, Anna and Simeon stood by the Savior and rejoiced that the promised Messiah had been born, bringing redemption to the world. What a tragedy that so many sincere people went to God's house that day but failed to meet God's Son!

Anna set a good example for us to follow, not only during the Christmas season but each day of the year.

For one thing, *her life was focused on the Lord*. We don't have to go to sacred buildings to worship the Lord, because God doesn't live in man-made temples, even the ones that are dedicated to Him. Certainly we ought to meet regularly to worship the Lord with God's people (Heb. 10:25), but each day we must also have times of worship and praise, beginning with the morning hour. No matter how we feel or how many pills we have to take each morning, let's lift our hearts in praise to God for all His mercies. "In the morning, Lord, you hear my voice; in the morning I lay my requests before you and wait expectantly" (Ps. 5:3).

That word "expectantly" reminds us of a second characteristic of Anna that is worthy of our imitation: *her life was motivated by hope.* Many elderly saints have a tendency to live in the past tense, in a world they like to call "the good old days," but Anna lived with her eyes on the future. Memories of past blessings are wonderful and should be cultivated, but we cannot live in the past, even though the past lives in us. Each day as she worshiped in the temple, Anna said in her heart, *Perhaps today! Perhaps today!* God's people should be motivated by the expectation of Jesus' coming again. At the Christmas season, we don't worship a baby in a manger. We worship a glorified Lord enthroned in heaven, and He has promised to come again! We are waiting for "the blessed hope and glorious appearing of our great God and Savior, Jesus Christ" (Titus 2:13 NKJV).

Anna practiced *spiritual disciplines.* She fasted and prayed and worshiped the Lord no matter how she felt or what disappointments came into her life. The older we grow, the more we need physical disciplines so that we don't harm God's temple (our body), but we need spiritual disciplines even more. "For physical training is of some value," Paul wrote to Timothy, "but godliness has value for all things, holding promise for both the present life and the life to come" (1 Tim. 4:8). What the apostle John desired for his dear friend Gaius ought to be our desire: "I pray that you may enjoy good health and that all may go well with you, even as your soul is getting along well" (3 John 1:2).

Anna was *a thankful believer.* If you asked her how she felt, she didn't give you a medical history but just praised the Lord for His goodness. She had never heard of the apostle Paul, but she practiced what he wrote in 1 Thessalonians 5:16—"Rejoice always, pray continually, give thanks in all circumstances; for this is God's will for you in Christ Jesus."

Anna was *a witness*. She wasn't afraid to tell others about the Lord. She also encouraged that small group of faithful Jewish believers—the "remnant"—who expectantly awaited the coming of the promised Messiah.

And what was the secret of this woman's faith and faithfulness? The grace of God. The name Anna comes from the Hebrew name Hannah and means "grace." She could say with Paul, "But by the grace of God I am what I am" (1 Cor. 15:10). Grace is God's generous favor to the undeserving because of what Jesus did for us on the cross. We don't deserve grace and we cannot earn it; all we can do is receive it by faith and say, "Thank You, Lord."

No doubt you have heard people say, or perhaps you have said yourself, "Christmas is for children." Take a long look at this group standing in the temple and you will never say it again. You have Mary, Joseph, Simeon, Anna—and Jesus, the center of their hearts' attention. Mary was a teenager, Joseph was perhaps twice as old as his wife, and Simeon and Anna were aged; but they were all united around the Savior. There were no generation gaps, for when Jesus is Lord of our lives, He turns "the hearts of the fathers to their children and the hearts of the children to their fathers" (Mal. 4:6 NASB). He bridges the generations and brings them together.

"Christmas is for children" certainly wasn't true at that first Christmastime, because Jesus was welcomed and worshiped by angels and shepherds, common people and sages, and especially by the older folks who had long been awaiting His coming. Christmas is for children, if by "children" you mean the humble of heart, regardless of age. "Truly I tell you," said Jesus, "unless you change and become like little children, you will never enter the kingdom of heaven" (Matt. 18:3).

He was describing Anna. Is He describing us?

ĉ See: Faith, Hope, Patience, Simeon

BABY

"A baby is God's opinion that the world should go on," wrote poet Carl Sandburg in his book *Remembrance Rock*. But there are people who dislike babies. One writer called babies "an alimentary canal with a loud voice at one end and no responsibility at the other." She forgot that we all got our start by being born, and if it hadn't been for caring people who received us, we would not have survived into adolescence and adulthood. Let's not be too critical of babies.

The Jewish theologians knew that their Messiah was to be born into the tribe of Judah, although they wished that He would come some other way. The first messianic prophecy in their Scriptures calls the promised Redeemer the "offspring" or "seed" of the woman (Gen. 3:15). The Magi asked where the king of the Jews was to be born, and the chief priests and teachers knew the answer—in Bethlehem of Judea (Matt. 2:1–6; Mic. 5:2). The king the Magi were searching for wasn't a conqueror on a throne. He was a child in His mother's arms.

If a twenty-first-century public relations firm had been assigned to program the coming of Jesus into the world, the staff would probably not have opted for the birth of a baby in a smelly cattle stall. A hero leading a victorious army would receive much better news coverage, or a radiant figure descending from heaven in clouds of glory; but Jesus came as a baby. In His birth, His life, and His death, Jesus failed to live up to the expectations of society, and society today is still disappointed. Imagine, God coming as a baby!

Society Worships Bigness

Which city has the tallest building, the biggest stadium or arena, the largest population? Who pastors the biggest church? Which nation has the biggest army? Who manages the biggest budget? When God planned to send salvation into the world, He chose to send His Son as something small—a baby. And He arranged for Him to be born in the "little town of Bethlehem," a village the prophet Micah called "small among the clans of Judah" (Mic. 5:2).

But small is powerful. When God wanted to establish the Jewish nation, the channel through which His Son would enter the world, He sent a little baby to a barren elderly couple. That son, Isaac, fathered Jacob and Jacob fathered the boys who grew up and founded the twelve tribes of Israel. God deigns to be called "the God of Abraham and of Isaac and of Jacob." It all started with a baby.

When His people were in bondage in Egypt and God needed a deliverer, He sent a baby boy to a devout Jewish couple, and Moses grew up to become that deliverer. Several generations after Israel had conquered Canaan, the people turned to idols and the light of God's truth grew dim. God sent a baby boy to Hannah and Elkanah, and Samuel grew up to lead the nation back to God. God brought two widows to Bethlehem—Naomi and Ruth—and Ruth married Boaz and in time gave birth to Obed. Two generations later, Obed's grandson David was born, and God used him to reestablish the kingdom that King Saul had almost destroyed. Jesus would be born of the family of

David. Yes, babies are small, but they are God's best answers to the needs of the world.

Society Worships Power

The people of Israel were under the iron fist of the Roman Empire and had no freedom or power. Throughout the centuries, a godly Jewish remnant had prayed for the Deliverer to come and bring the power they needed to find freedom. Finally, He came—as a baby!

But look carefully at the demonstration of that baby's power. Because of Jesus, Caesar Augustus had to issue a decree that would bring Mary and Joseph from Nazareth to Bethlehem, where the prophet said He would be born. Because of Jesus, a host of angels came from heaven to welcome His birth with their praises. He drew the shepherds from their flocks to the manger where they worshiped Him. Because of baby Jesus, a wonderful star moved from its place to guide the Magi to the home where He was, and they gave Him gifts. So powerful was this baby that His birth greatly disturbed Herod the Great and stirred the whole city of Jerusalem.

But Jesus is no longer a baby in a manger. He is the exalted King of Kings and Lord of Lords, "far above all rule and authority, power and dominion, and every title that can be given" (Eph. 1:21). *Every* title, including president, king, emperor, emir, Mikado, raja, shah, sultan, czar, CEO, Führer, duke, earl, baron, senator, congressman, member of Parliament, maharajah, Secretary of State, Lord High Commissioner, mayor, and even Caesar. The authority of Jesus is the greatest of all.

When we claim His promises, when we yield to His Holy Spirit, when we pray and when we obey, we share in that authority and accomplish His purposes on this earth. "In this world you will have trouble," He told His disciples. "But take heart! I have overcome the world" (John 16:33). The world looks at Christians as inferior underlings, but Jesus sees us as unbeatable overcomers.

Society Worships Wealth

Babies are rich in potential but poor in possessions, no matter how many lovely gifts people may bring them. A baby cannot own property, inherit an estate, or sign a check. Babies don't even know they are babies. In time, they learn who their parents and siblings are and what the family is worth, but not a cent is theirs until they are old enough to inherit.

Jesus wasn't born in a comfortable house, surrounded by loving people. He was born in a cattle stall surrounded by strangers and farm animals. His foster father, Joseph, was a carpenter, a man too poor to bring a lamb for a sacrifice (Luke 2:21–24). When Jesus was grown and busy in ministry, He had no place of His own to lay His head. He borrowed boats so He could travel. He borrowed a little boy's lunch so He could feed a crowd of thousands, He borrowed a donkey for His "Palm Sunday" presentation in Jerusalem, and He borrowed an upper room for His last Passover. He even borrowed a tomb so He could be properly buried after dying on the cross.

"For you know the grace of our Lord Jesus Christ," wrote the apostle Paul, "that though he was rich, yet for your sakes he became poor, so that you through his poverty might become rich" (2 Cor. 8:9). He was rich in heaven and became poor on earth so that we who are poor might trust Him and receive heavenly riches. What a paradox! And the spiritual riches we have in Christ never lose their value, cannot be stolen from us, and keep multiplying to enrich our lives more and more. God's children share the riches of His wisdom (Rom. 11:33), grace (Eph. 1:7; 2:7), and mercy (2:4); in fact, the riches they have in Christ are so vast they are unsearchable (3:8). Paul described believers as "poor, yet making many rich" (2 Cor. 6:10), and Jesus said to the suffering saints in Smyrna, "I know your afflictions and your poverty—yet you are rich!" (Rev. 2:9).

The riches of this world are uncertain (1 Tim. 6:17), but the riches we have in Christ are eternal.

Society Wants Instant Results

"Ears pierced while you wait." The jeweler who put that sign in his store window didn't know much about writing but he certainly understood his customers. Most people today belong to the Now Generation and what they want must be delivered immediately. Instant gratification and prompt performance are absolute essentials or they will take their business elsewhere.

But the Lord doesn't operate that way. He can grow a mushroom overnight, but it takes decades to grow the mighty oak and centuries for a sequoia. He waited twenty-five years before He sent baby Isaac to Abraham and Sarah, and more than four hundred years before He sent Moses to deliver Israel from Egypt. Centuries passed before the promise of Genesis 3:15 was fulfilled in the birth of Jesus, and how many years have come and gone since Jesus promised to come again? The sooner we learn that God isn't in a hurry, the more peace we will have in our hearts and the more effective our lives will be. We don't want to follow the hyperactive crowds around us. We want to "imitate those who through faith and patience inherit what has been promised" (Heb. 6:12).

The word for this priceless attitude is *hope*. When new parents look lovingly on their precious baby, their hearts are filled with hope, for every baby is a vote for the future. The question that was asked about eight-day-old John the Baptist may be asked about any new baby: "What then is this child going to be?" (Luke 1:66). Unfortunately, there are people today who consider babies nuisances, and some of them don't hesitate to interrupt the hidden miracle occurring in a mother's womb. The Jewish people have always welcomed babies and valued them. "Sons are a heritage of the LORD, children a reward from him," wrote King Solomon. "Like arrows in the hands of a warrior are sons born in one's youth. Blessed is the man whose quiver is full of them" (Ps. 127:3–5). David said that daughters were "like pillars carved to adorn a palace" (144:12). Proverbs 17:6 reminds grandparents, "Children's children are a crown to the aged."

Dr. Luke recorded the story of our Lord's conception, birth, and presentation in the temple, and then skipped to His twelfth year and then to His thirtieth year when He began His public ministry (Luke 2:41–52; 3:23). Were those unmentioned years unimportant years? Of course not! They were simply unrecorded years, a time when the Father was preparing His Son for three years of sacrificial ministry, climaxing in the cross, the resurrection, and the ascension. The Father didn't think it a waste of time to invest thirty years in equipping His Son for the most important work ever accomplished on this planet. The Father's words after Jesus' baptism tell us that Jesus successfully passed every test: "This is my Son, whom I love; with him I am well pleased" (Matt. 3:17).

The beautiful words of Phillips Brooks come to mind.

> O holy Child of Bethlehem,
>   Descend to us, we pray;
> Cast out our sin and enter in,
>   Be born in us today.
> We hear the Christmas angels
>   The great glad tidings tell;
> O come to us, abide with us,
>   Our Lord Immanuel.

֎ **See: Immanuel, Virgin Birth**

BETHLEHEM

The Bible mentions two towns named Bethlehem, one seven miles northwest of Nazareth in Zebulun (Josh. 19:15; Judg. 12:8–10), and the other five miles southwest of Jerusalem in Judah, the Bethlehem where Jesus was born. *That* Bethlehem is mentioned nearly thirty times in the Old Testament and has a rich history that relates directly to Jesus Christ and helps us better understand Him and what He came to do for us.

Bread

Bethlehem means "house of bread," and *Ephrathah* means "fruitful," because the land around Bethlehem was very productive. It was common knowledge among the Jews that the Messiah would be born in Bethlehem (John 7:42). Seven centuries before Jesus was born, the prophet Micah wrote, "But you, Bethlehem Ephrathah, though you are small among the clans of Judah, out of you will come for me one who will be ruler over Israel, whose origins are from of old, from ancient times" (Mic. 5:2).

That Jesus, the Bread of Life (John 6:33–40), should be born in the "house of bread" is no accident. The Father sent manna from heaven to sustain the people of Israel in the wilderness but He sent Jesus to *give life to the whole world*. It cost the Lord nothing to send the manna each morning, but it cost Jesus His life on the cross to give the bread of life to a world of lost sinners. Eat the bread of this world and you will always hunger, but receive Jesus and feed on Him and you will never hunger. His earthly life as the incarnate Son of God began at "the house of bread," and our eternal life begins when we trust Jesus Christ, the Bread of Life.

Sorrow

When Jacob and his family were traveling back home to his father, Isaac, Jacob's beloved wife Rachel died in childbirth near Bethlehem, then called Ephrath (Gen. 35:16–20). She gave birth to a son whom she named Ben-Oni, "son of my trouble," but Jacob gave his son a different name, Benjamin, "son of my right hand." Rachel already had one son, Joseph, and she had previously said to Jacob, "Give me children, or I'll die!" (Gen. 30:1). God took her at her word.

Jesus is Ben-Oni, "a man of sorrows, and familiar with suffering" (Isa. 53:3). But He is also Benjamin, "the Son of God's right hand." Ben-Oni speaks of suffering, but Benjamin speaks of glory. He could not be glorified until first He was crucified. Jesus identified with the sorrows and suffering of this world and today He gives grace and mercy when we come to His throne and ask in faith (Heb. 4:14–16).

Love

One of the greatest love stories in history is that of Ruth and Boaz, and it takes place in the town of Bethlehem. The account is recorded in the Bible in the book of Ruth. Ruth and her mother-in-law, Naomi, both of them widows, came to Bethlehem where they hoped somehow to begin a new life. While Ruth was gleaning in the harvest fields, Boaz, the lord of the harvest, saw her and fell in love with her. He was a wealthy near kinsman to her deceased husband and was therefore able to redeem her from her poverty. They married, and God sent them a baby boy whom they named Obed, who ultimately was the grandfather of David the king.

Jesus is our Lord of the harvest. He loves us and paid the price to redeem us from our spiritual poverty. "Christ loved the church and gave himself up for her" (Eph. 5:25). Salvation isn't a commercial transaction; it's a love relationship between the believer and the Savior. Love came down to Bethlehem to set us free from our sins.

Thirst

A neglected but important event in the life of David is recorded in 2 Samuel 23:13–17. While Saul was king and David was in exile, David was with his men in the cave of Adullam and longed for a drink of water from the well in his boyhood home of Bethlehem. He didn't issue an order; he simply said under his breath, "Oh, that someone would get me a drink of water from the well near the gate of Bethlehem!" The Philistines held Bethlehem at that time, but three of David's mighty men, wanting to please their leader, broke through the lines, secured the water, and brought it to David. But David refused to drink it. "Is it not the blood of men who went at the risk of their lives?" he said, and he poured it out as a drink offering to the Lord.

Bethlehem is not only a house of bread but also a place where spiritual thirst is quenched. Jesus said to the woman at Jacob's well in Samaria, "Everyone who drinks this water will be thirsty again, but whoever drinks the water I give him will never thirst" (John 4:13). The last invitation in the Bible says, "Whoever is thirsty, let him come; and whoever wishes, let him take the free gift of the water of life" (Rev. 22:17). Jesus came to Bethlehem to satisfy the thirst in the heart of everyone who is tired of the cheap substitutes the world offers.

Hope

For forty years the prophet Jeremiah had warned the people of Jerusalem and Judah that judgment was coming, but the people refused to obey and abandon their idols. The Babylonian army did arrive, looting and destroying the city and the temple. They also took thousands of Jewish exiles to Babylon.

The town of Ramah, about five miles north of Jerusalem, was one of the stopping points for the exiles. Jeremiah gave them this message from the Lord: "A voice is heard in Ramah, mourning and great weeping, Rachel weeping for her children and refusing to be comforted, because her children are no more" (Jer. 31:15). As they trudged along, the people would recall Rachel's death at Bethlehem when she was giving birth to Benjamin. She died to bring Benjamin into the world, and now his descendants were going into exile. Was it worth it? Matthew quoted this verse and applied it to the slaughter of the little boys in Bethlehem (Matt. 2:16–18).

But Jeremiah didn't stop simply with noting the sorrow of the exiles. He also promised them that Israel would return to their land and establish the nation and the temple again. "This is what the LORD says: 'Restrain your voice from weeping and your eyes from tears, for your work will be rewarded,' declares the LORD. 'They will return from the land of the enemy. So there is hope for your future,' declares the LORD. 'Your children will return to their own land'" (Jer. 31:16–17). God kept His promise and the nation was restored.

If Jesus had not been born there, the town of Bethlehem would have been remembered only for tragic events—the death of Rachel, the exile of the people of Judah, the death of the innocent little boys. But Jesus Christ is "our hope" (1 Tim. 1:1), and God "has given us new birth into a living hope through the resurrection of Jesus Christ from the dead" (1 Pet. 1:3). The Advent season is a time of joy because it is a time of hope. If the promises were fulfilled when Jesus came the first time, surely the promises of His second coming will also be fulfilled.

𝒆 See: David, Herod the Great, Innocents

CAESAR

Caesar Augustus ruled over the Roman Empire at the time Jesus was born. Augustus was Gaius Julius Caesar Octavianus, the adopted son of Julius Caesar. He was awarded the title Augustus by the Roman Senate; the title meant "revered" and implied that its bearer was divine. While he had the power of a dictator, Augustus styled himself the "First Citizen." He ruled from 27 BC to AD 14.

Realizing that some areas of the empire required a military presence, Augustus placed Roman troops in volatile Palestine (which included Judea, Galilee, Samaria, Idumea, and lesser entities). He is the one who put in motion the tax cycle that brought Mary and Joseph to Bethlehem (Luke 2:1). At the time of his death, Augustus was admired by the Romans for bringing peace and prosperity to the empire.

While Caesar has an indirect role in the birth of Christ, his presence in the account invites us to reflect on the plan of God in relation to those in power. The sovereignty of God rules the kings of the earth. "The king's heart is like channels of water in the hand of the LORD; He turns it wherever He wishes" (Prov. 21:1 NASB).

Micah had prophesied that Messiah would be born in Bethlehem (Mic. 5:2). By issuing the order that a census be taken throughout the Roman Empire, Augustus provided the reason for Mary and Joseph to travel from Nazareth to Bethlehem. And there the Word of the Lord was proved true. There is a mystery in how God's providence shapes the choices of human agents, but the lesson is that God fulfills His purposes according to His Word.

Those in positions of political or financial power may not realize it, but ultimately they serve God's purposes. Rulers may be a blessing or a threat to God's people, but God rules over the nations (see Rom. 13:1–7). The persons in power are not as powerful as they may think.

Augustus Caesar was deified by decree of the Roman senate after his death. The divinity that had been previously implied was now made explicit. One of the early church's greatest challenges was a test of loyalty. The state wanted its citizens to declare "Caesar is Lord." Faithful Christians chose to say only, "Jesus is Lord."

𝒆 See: Bethlehem, John the Baptist

CHRISTMAS

A Word

Let's think first of Christmas as a word. The English word *Christmas* dates from before the twelfth century. In Old English it was two words, *Christes maesse*, and in Middle English, *Christemasse*. Literally it meant "Christ's mass" and referred to the special worship service held on December 25 in honor of the birth of the Lord Jesus Christ.

"Christmas" as cited in Noah Webster's American Dictionary of the English Language, 1828, reads: "[Christ and mass] The festival of the christian church observed annually on the 25th day of December, in memory of the birth of Christ" (spelling follows the original citation).

That the first syllable of Christmas comes from the word "Christ" is indisputable. In Greek the name Christ is χριστός (*christos*). The first letter looks like the English letter X. Every vocation has its shorthand, and those in the church used the letter chi (χ) to represent Christ in words that began with "Christ-." So "Xmas" is an honorable abbreviation for Christmas. It was not intended to take Christ out of Christmas (although in these politically correct days some want to do just that).

A Season

Now consider Christmas as a season. In terms of the economy, the Christmas season begins right after Labor Day, when trees and decorations appear in the big box stores. It used to start after Thanksgiving. Whenever the season starts, it points to December 25.

The best reason historians can offer for observing Christmas on December 25 is that it was the day the Romans celebrated the "birthday of the unconquered sun," following the Saturnalia festival (December 17–24). The longer days following the winter solstice were significant in a world lit only by fire. In the mid–fourth century, the Roman church imposed a Christian celebration over the pagan day, calling it the Feast of the Nativity of the Sun of Righteousness (part of the name was taken from Malachi 4:2).

Initially the Church celebrated the birth of Christ, the coming of the shepherds, and the adoration of the Magi on January 6, a day also associated with the Lord's baptism. By AD 336, December 25 was recognized in Rome as the day of Christ's birth (although December 25 was in use by the early 200s). By the sixth century, the entire Western Church had moved the celebration of the nativity to December 25, along with the shepherds' visit and adoration of the Magi. The Eastern Church continues to link the adoration of the wise men with Epiphany, January 6. Jesus might have been born in late December or early January, but we can't know for sure.

Over time, Christmas became a festive season that lasted until Epiphany, giving us the twelve days of Christmas (the twelve days begin with the day after Christmas). For Christians, the giving and receiving of gifts follows the example of the Magi. The use of lights reflects both the increasing natural light of the time of year and the growing spiritual light of Christ, who is the Light of the World.

Some Christmas customs in the United States come from European traditions, such as decorating with greens and enjoying a feast (or two). The Puritan settlers in New England took a dim view of Christmas, in part because it had been marked by drunkenness in the mother country. So Christmas was banned in Massachusetts by law and violators were fined five shillings.

Given today's climate of political correctness, there is annual debate about what greeting to use during the season: "Happy Holidays!" or "Season's Greetings!" instead of "Merry Christmas!" Schools have had to change their Christmas Concert to a Winter Celebration. Followers of Jesus will use the vocabulary that best expresses the spiritual truth of the season.

A Historic Event

Christmas is also a historic event. By AD 120 Roman historians mention "Christ" several times but without detail. His crucifixion is specifically mentioned. Since he died, obviously Jesus was born. His birth in Bethlehem, to a virgin mother, was the fulfillment of biblical prophecy.

Mary and Joseph made the trip to Bethlehem to register for Caesar's census, decreed by the governor of Syria (Luke 2:1–2). There is no record of a universal census under Augustus, but during his reign, he required a census in many parts of the empire, and the decree mentioned by Luke may have been specifically to include the Jews. A Jewish census would have required returning to a family's roots. God shapes human events, and a ruler's decree was the means by which God kept His Word.

The tale of the mean innkeeper who refused Mary and Joseph a room and forced them into a cave or barn is woven into the fabric of the Christmas story, but it isn't true. Bethlehem would have been crowded with people registering for the census, and most visitors would have stayed with relatives. The word *inn* in Luke 2:7 is an unfortunate translation; it would be better rendered "guest room." Probably Bethlehem did not have a "motel" or inn because it was off the main trade routes.

In those days most families kept animals in the lower level of the house; thus a manger would be a normal furnishing there. The lower level was divided, animals on one side, the family sleeping space on the other. Since the guest room was full, Mary probably gave birth in that lower level room and used the manger as Jesus' cradle.

Herod the Great was king in Judea at the time of Jesus' birth. One of Herod's final atrocities was to have the boys under age two in Bethlehem put to the sword (Matt. 2:16). The Jews considered a child who reached the age of one to be two years old (first "year" in the womb). Herod died between 4 and 1 BC, so Jesus had to have been born at least a year before Herod's death.

Luke tells us that the shepherds were with their flocks in the fields near Bethlehem (2:8). Normally sheep would be in pasture from spring to fall, but near Bethlehem sheep may have been outdoors in wintertime as well. If so, it is possible that Jesus was born in December in a year prior to 1 BC, but this cannot be proven.

A Spiritual Experience

Most important, Christmas should be a spiritual experience. Jesus came to earth to save sinners (Matt. 1:21). The angel's announcement to the shepherds was "for all the people" (Luke 2:10). Christmas is not just an event in time; it is a spiritual experience available to every person who hears the gospel. Jesus was physically born in Bethlehem so He could be spiritually born in the hearts of those who believe in Him. Jesus is God's gift to the human race.

John tells us that Jesus "came to His own, and those who were His own did not receive Him. But as many as received Him, to them He gave the right to become children of God, even to those who believe in His name" (John 1:11–12 NASB). Jesus still looks for those who will receive Him. Receiving Jesus means believing that He is God's Son who became human, lived a sinless life, died for our sins, and rose to live forever. Receiving Jesus means receiving the gift of salvation. That is the experience of Christmas.

When we are born again, we begin a new kind of life. Knowing Jesus as Savior brings joy to our heart, peace to our mind, and worship to our soul. Being a follower of Jesus gives purpose and meaning to life. Because Jesus meets our needs, we are able to serve others in His name. He understands what it's like to grow up, work hard, be hungry, experience pain, and die. Jesus makes our ultimate destiny sure: His presence in heaven in a glorified human body is the guarantee that redeemed humans will one day be there with Him.

Have you received the gift of salvation?

> O holy Child of Bethlehem,
>   Descend to us, we pray;
> Cast out our sin and enter in,
>   Be born in us today.
>
> *Phillips Brooks*

❧ See: Bethlehem, Caesar, Epiphany, Herod the Great, Inn, Innocents, Manger, Wise Men, Xmas

DAVID

King David is mentioned more than one thousand times in the Bible, including thirty-eight times in the four Gospels. David cannot be left out of the birth narrative of Jesus.

Consider the important links between David and the birth of the Savior.

The Name of David

Son of David was one of the popular names of Jesus in the Gospel records, and during His ministry, people debated whether or not He was the promised Messiah. Matthew opens his Gospel with, "A record of the genealogy of Jesus Christ the son of David" (Matt. 1:1). "What do you think about the Christ?" Jesus asked some of the Pharisees. "Whose son is he?" They replied, "The son of David," and they were right (22:41–42). In the Hebrew language, the name David means "beloved." The Father called Jesus His "beloved" at His baptism (Matt. 3:17; Mark 1:11; Luke 3:22 NASB) and at the transfiguration (Matt. 17:5; Mark 9:7 NASB). See also Luke 20:13 NASB.

Like David, Jesus was rejected and had to suffer before He was crowned king; and, as in David's family, our Lord's own brothers didn't accept Him until later (1 Sam. 17:27–31; 22:1; John 7:1–9). Both David and Jesus won victories in private before they displayed their power in public (1 Sam. 17:33–37; Matt. 4:1–11).

The Family of David

Jesus' mother Mary belonged to the family of David (Luke 3:31) and so did His foster father Joseph (2:4, and see 1:69). There was no Jewish monarchy in those days (Hosea 3:4–5), but there were descendants of David who still remained faithful to the Lord. "I am the Root and the Offspring of David," Jesus said to John in Revelation 22:16. See also Revelation 5:5. As the "Root of David," Jesus brought the family of David into being, for He is God; and as the "Offspring of David," He became man and was born of Mary, a descendant of David. Paul explained that "as to his human nature [Jesus] was a descendant of David, and . . . through the Spirit of holiness was declared with power to be the Son of God" (Rom. 1:3–4).

In Romans 15:12 Jesus is called "the Root of Jesse." Jesse was David's father. The promise is given that Jesus will one day reign over His kingdom on earth. Whenever God's people pray, "Your kingdom come," they are asking for this promise to be fulfilled. The apostle Paul, a devout Jew, emphasized the Jewish ancestry of Jesus, knowing that the future of the promised kingdom depended on this (Acts 28:20). "Remember Jesus Christ, raised from the dead, descended from David" (2 Tim. 2:8). Why remember that Jesus descended from David? Because the promises God made to David about his royal throne will one day be fulfilled in Jesus Christ, David's greatest son.

The Town of David

To comply with the Roman census, Joseph and Mary left Nazareth and traveled seventy-five miles to Bethlehem, "the town of David," and there Jesus was born (Luke 2:1–7). This would not have been an easy journey for Mary, and the situation didn't improve when they learned there was no room for them in the inn.

As we noted in our remarks on Bethlehem, the town would have been remembered for the place where Rachel died, but today, because of Jesus, it's remembered as the place where the Savior was born. The wise men were sure that a great king would be born in Jerusalem, but the prophet Micah pointed them to Bethlehem (Mic. 5:2), the town of David.

The Throne of David

God's promise to Mary was, "The Lord God will give him [Jesus] the throne of his father David, and he will reign over the house of Jacob forever; his kingdom will never end" (Luke 1:32–33). But for centuries Israel has had no king. The prophet Hosea foretold these days: "For the Israelites will live many days without king or prince" (Hosea 3:4). "We have no king but Caesar," the chief priests told Pilate (John 19:15), and so Israel rejected her only lawful king.

God had promised David, "Your house and your kingdom will endure forever before me; your throne will be established forever" (2 Sam. 7:16). This promise was never fulfilled in any of David's successors, but it will be fulfilled in Jesus Christ. Today He is seated on the Father's throne, but Hosea 3:5 promises, "Afterward the Israelites will return and seek the LORD their God and David their king. They will come trembling to the LORD and to his blessings in the last days." Jeremiah wrote, "'In that day,' declares the LORD Almighty, 'I will break the yoke off their necks and will tear off their bonds; no longer will foreigners enslave them. Instead, they will serve the LORD their God and David their king, whom I will raise up for them'" (Jer. 30:8–9).

These verses refer to the establishment of the kingdom promised to Israel, when Jesus will reign and "the government will be on his shoulders. . . . He will reign on David's throne and over his kingdom, establishing and upholding it with justice and righteousness from that time on and forever" (Isa. 9:6–7; and see Isaiah 11). "I will maintain my love to him forever, and my covenant with him will never fail. I will establish his line forever, his throne as long as the heavens endure" (Ps. 89:28–29). Only Jesus Christ, the eternal Son of God, could fulfill this promise that God made to David. Read what Peter told the Jews at Pentecost in Acts 2:29–36.

Mary understood the national ramifications of the coming of Jesus (Luke 1:54–55) and so did Zechariah (vv. 67–75). Jesus came as a Jew to the Jews, and they in turn took the gospel message to the Gentiles, so that through Israel all the peoples of the earth could be blessed (Gen. 12:3; Gal. 3:8). Here's how Paul expressed it: "For I tell you that Christ has become a servant of the Jews on behalf of God's truth, to confirm the promises made to the patriarchs so that the Gentiles may glorify God for his mercy" (Rom. 15:8–9).

If anybody has reason to glorify God at the Christmas season, it's the Gentiles who were outside the covenants and the promises and yet brought near and brought in by Jesus Christ (Eph. 2:11–22).

The Key of David

"These are the words of him who is holy and true, who holds the key of David. What he opens no one can shut, and what he shuts no one can open" (Rev. 3:7). A key is a symbol of authority, and "the key of David" relates to Christ's authority over the house of David in fulfilling the promises God made to Israel.

Ancient locks and keys were much different from their modern equivalents. We insert metal keys that move the bolts horizontally in the locks, but the ancients had large wooden keys that were pulled vertically. This pushed up the iron bolts and unlocked the door. The person who carried this key was the most important person in the palace, next to the king, and everyone did his bidding. Jesus holds not only the key of David but also the keys of death and Hades (Rev. 1:18). He is the one who has the authority.

The background for this image is recorded in Isaiah 22:15–25. Shebna was in charge of the palace; he was the man with the key. But he selfishly used his authority for his own purposes, including having an elaborate tomb cut out for him at the king's expense. But the prophet Isaiah told him he wouldn't be honored with a great, royal funeral but would die an exile in a foreign land and be buried there. Eliakim was appointed in his place and given the key and he was a faithful steward who brought honor to the Lord and to the king.

The Jewish rabbis saw Eliakim as a picture of Jesus Christ, the faithful steward over the house (family) of David. The church in Philadelphia was given great opportunities for ministry, doors that the Lord opened for them that nobody could close (Rev. 3:7–8). Jesus had the key and He determined what the church should do. There was in Philadelphia a "synagogue of Satan" that claimed to be Christian but was actually made up of counterfeit Christians, and Jesus would deal with them. Jesus has the key—the authority—and we must listen to Him and obey Him. If He closes a door, we must not try to pry it open.

While the spiritual application of this passage belongs to all Christians and encourages us to be faithful stewards, we must not forget the basic interpretation to the people of Israel. They rejected Jesus but He is still in charge of their future and will fulfill the covenants and promises that He gave them. There are believers who say there is no future for Israel, but as long as Jesus holds the key of David, nobody can close the door.

The Music of David

David was a remarkable combination of shepherd, soldier, administrator, poet, and musician. Nearly half of the psalms are attributed to David, and many of those we call messianic psalms because they speak of Jesus Christ. Jesus said, "Everything must be fulfilled that is written about me in the Law of Moses, the Prophets and the Psalms" (Luke 24:44).

The book of Psalms was the official hymnal of the Jewish people, and those like Simeon and Anna who looked forward to the coming of Messiah found encouragement for their faith as they sang these inspired songs. Psalm 2 spoke to them of the King who would reign and conquer their enemies (see Heb. 1:5; Acts 13:33). Psalm 22 describes the crucifixion and resurrection of Christ (see Matt. 27:35, 39, 43, 45–46; John 19:23–24, 28; Heb. 2:12), and the familiar Psalm 23 describes His shepherding ministry to His people (John 10). Psalm 110:4 presents Jesus as the "priest forever in the order of Melchizedek" (Heb. 5:6, 10; 6:20; 7:17, 21), and verse 1 affirms the divine sonship of our Lord (Matt. 22:44–45; Luke 20:42–44). Psalm 16:8–11 anticipates the burial and resurrection of Jesus, verses Peter quoted in his sermon on the Day of Pentecost (Acts 2:25–28).

These are but a few examples of the messianic messages of the book of Psalms. King David wrote about the Son of David centuries before Jesus was born at Bethlehem, and the church is grateful that he did. "Israel's beloved singer" (2 Sam. 23:1 NIV Study Bible, margin note) sang about Jesus, and so should we.

𝑒 See: Immanuel, King, Messiah, Prophecy

DREAMS

The phrase "in a dream" is found six times in Matthew's Gospel, five times in the narrative of the birth of Jesus (1:20; 2:12, 13, 19, 22) and once in the account of the trial of Jesus (27:19). The dreams God gave to Joseph and the wise men were important parts of the birth drama and revealed God's loving care as He protected His Son and His servants from the enemy.

Occasionally in the Old Testament, the Lord spoke to people through dreams, and this included people outside the Jewish covenant, such as Abimelech (Gen. 20:3), Laban (31:24), a Midianite soldier (Judg. 7:13–15), Pharaoh and his butler and baker (Genesis 40–41), and King Nebuchadnezzar (Daniel 2, 4). God gave dreams to Jacob, founder of the twelve tribes of Israel (Gen. 28:12; 31:10–13), and to Jacob's son Joseph (37:1–11). Joseph's brothers scornfully nicknamed him "that dreamer" (v. 19), but it was Joseph whom God used to save the nation of Israel.

In the law of Moses, the Lord warned the Jewish people not to depend for guidance on the interpretation of dreams. Yes, a true prophet might receive a message from God in a dream, but only the Lord could give the correct interpretation (Num. 12:1–8; Deuteronomy 13; 18:9–22). The Israelites were to beware of false prophets and "dreamers" who would lead them astray (Jer. 23:25–40; 27:9–11; 29:1–9; Zech. 10:2). There is no evidence in Scripture that Israel had a guild of "dream experts."

Joseph, the husband of Mary, was given four dreams, each of which played an important part in the protection of Jesus. First, when Joseph learned that Mary was pregnant, he was perplexed over what to do, and God told him in a dream to go ahead and marry her and thereby give the baby a safe home and a name—Jesus, "Jehovah saves" (Matt. 1:18–25). In naming the baby, Joseph legally claimed Him, even though Joseph was only the foster father.

While King Herod was scheming to kill the newborn King of the Jews, God warned Joseph in a dream to flee to Egypt with Mary and the Child. There was a large Jewish settlement in Egypt, and they would be safe there. God also warned the wise men in a dream not to return to Herod but to go home by another route (2:1–18). After King Herod died, God directed Joseph in a dream to return to Judea, but when he heard that Herod's cruel son Archelaus was on the throne, he hesitated. In another dream, the Lord told him to go back home to Nazareth in Galilee (vv. 19–23), and he obeyed. Matthew saw in the trip to Egypt the fulfillment of Hosea 11:1.

The Lord spoke in dreams to Joseph and to the wise men because they had to act quickly at a time of great danger and there wasn't time to send a prophet to warn them, even if one had been available. (Israel had not heard a prophet for four hundred years.) The important thing was to protect Jesus from those who would kill Him. Joseph and the wise men obeyed God's commands and escaped the wrath of the king.

Does this mean that believers today should expect God to direct them through their dreams? Probably not. With two thousand years of Christian history behind us, an inspired Bible before us, the Holy Spirit within us, and loving Christians around us, believers today have the resources they need for making wise decisions. In the dreams mentioned in Matthew 1 and 2, the dreamers heard God speak either directly or through an angel, and no interpretation was necessary. The dreams were clear announcements, not puzzling enigmas. There were emergencies abroad and God was at work saving His people.

Many psychiatrists believe that dreams have their origin in the desires and fears we bury in our subconscious. They see dreams as coded messages from within that expose the self we want to hide; and once we "decode" the message, we are set free from our "false self" to become our "true self." Many people have been helped by skilled counselors who have guided them in facing reality and dealing with it honestly, an experience not unlike a Christian conversion experience but without the work of the Holy Spirit and the imparting of new life. But none of the dreams we examined in Matthew 1 and 2 fit into this category.

Missionaries tell us that dreams are playing a part today in their ministry to difficult people groups. People dream about Jesus or "a black book" (the Bible) and seek out Christians to explain their dreams, and many of these people come to faith in Christ. Wherever there are sincere people seeking truth, God can reveal Himself to them as He did to Abram in Ur of the Chaldeans (Acts 7:2–3) and Cornelius the Gentile soldier in Caesarea (Acts 10). The Lord adapts His methods to those He is seeking to reach, and if they only "touch the edge of his cloak" (Luke 8:43–48), He will graciously respond to even the weakest faith.

♪ See: Joseph, Wise Men

EGYPT

When King Herod heard from the wise men that a "king of the Jews" had been born, he was disturbed and determined to destroy Him, but God arranged for His Son to be protected in Egypt. He ordered the wise men not to return to Jerusalem and He warned Joseph and Mary to take the Child and flee to Egypt. When Herod realized that the wise men had outwitted him, he ordered his soldiers to kill all the boys in Bethlehem who were two years old and under. Since Bethlehem was a small town, it's likely that no more than fifteen or twenty boys were slain, but even one is too many. Simeon had told Mary that a sword would pierce her soul because of Jesus, and when she heard about the slaughter in Bethlehem, she must have remembered that prophecy (Luke 2:25–35).

Many centuries before, the Lord had told Jacob and his family to go to Egypt where Joseph would protect them (Genesis 46). Because Joseph had saved the nation from starvation, Pharaoh welcomed his family and provided for them. But when a new ruler and a new generation arose that didn't remember or revere Joseph, the Egyptians turned against the Jews and enslaved them. God raised up Moses and Aaron to deliver the Jews from Egyptian bondage (Exodus 12–14), and for centuries the Jews have celebrated this event at Passover.

It was about seventy-five miles from Bethlehem to Egypt, and once there, Joseph and his family would be out from under Herod's jurisdiction. There was a large Jewish population in Egypt and it's likely that Joseph and Mary found relatives there who would take them in. The gifts from the wise men would have helped to meet their expenses for the journey. After Herod died, the Lord told Joseph and Mary to return with the Child to their own land, and Matthew saw in this the fulfillment of Hosea 11:1, "Out of Egypt I called my son."

This suggests a parallel between the nation of Israel and the person of Jesus. Both are called "God's son" (Exod. 4:22–23; Deut. 1:31; 32:6; Matt. 3:17) and both were protected in Egypt and then called out. Israel began national life by passing through the Red Sea ("baptized into Moses"—1 Cor. 10:1–2), and Jesus began His public ministry by being baptized in the Jordan River by John the Baptist (Matt. 3:13–17). After the exodus from Egypt, Israel went into the wilderness where God tested them (Deut. 8:2), and Jesus went into the wilderness after His baptism where Satan tempted Him (Matt. 4:1–11). Israel failed miserably, but the Lord Jesus was triumphant.

Bible geography tells us not only *where* events occurred but often *why* they occurred. Israel is the people of God, but Egypt typifies the world and its opposition to God's people. To Israel, Egypt was a place of slavery and persecution, just as believers today suffer opposition from the world (John 16:33). The land of Canaan was Israel's God-given inheritance and He delivered Israel from Egypt that He might take them into Canaan. To Christian believers today, Canaan represents our rich inheritance in Jesus Christ, the victorious life of faith described in the Epistle to the Hebrews.

But Israel didn't believe God; instead of claiming their inheritance in Canaan, they rebelled and planned to go back to Egypt (see Numbers 13–14). God disciplined them by making them remain in the wilderness for thirty-eight more years until that unbelieving generation died off. The wilderness represents the aimless life of unbelief and disobedience that Christians experience when they refuse to trust God's promises and obey His will. Jesus said that believers are not of the world but are hated by the world even as He was hated (John 17:14–16).

Like Israel and our Lord Jesus Christ, Christians have been called out of Egypt—the world—because their citizenship is in heaven (Phil. 3:20–21) and they have been rescued "from the present evil age" (Gal. 1:3–5). But we are not to isolate ourselves from the world, because Jesus has sent us back into the world to share His gospel with the lost (John 17:11, 14–18). One day He will return and call us out of the world to spend eternity with Him (1 Thess. 4:13–18).

♪ See: Herod the Great, Jesus, Joseph, Mary, Questions

ELIJAH

The prophet Elijah stepped onto the stage of Scripture with no introduction. His style was direct and confrontational; there was no finesse in Elijah. He was a man devoted to God and he hated the idolatry that plagued Israel. His faith and courage were almost unshakeable.

The wilderness was Elijah's home. His clothing was suited to that environment but was not the height of fashion: he wore a garment of hair with a leather belt around his waist (2 Kings 1:8). Elijah's values were old-fashioned: worship Jehovah, obey His law, pursue justice, and do right. He was truly countercultural, resisting the false gods and those who worshiped them, which brought him into conflict with rulers.

Elijah's first confrontation with King Ahab was over the king's leading Israel to worship Baal (see 1 Kings 16:29–33). As God's representative, Elijah declared there would be no more rain until he said so (17:1). Judgment came on Israel through a three-and-a-half-year drought. At the showdown on Mt. Carmel between the priests of Baal and Elijah, Elijah prayed down fire from heaven on his sacrifice and then killed 450 priests of Baal. Then he prayed, and the rains came (1 Kings 18; James 5:17–18). When Ahab had his neighbor Naboth murdered to take his property, Elijah confronted the evil king again, predicting Ahab's line would be cut off because he sold himself "to do evil in the eyes of the LORD" (1 Kings 21:20–22; 22:34–40). Twice Elijah called down fire on the soldiers of King Ahaziah, and he predicted the king's death (2 Kings 1:1–17).

God ended Elijah's life on earth by taking him to heaven in a whirlwind (2:1–12). He appeared with Jesus at His transfiguration (Matt. 17:3). Malachi 4:5 states that Elijah will appear again before the Day of the Lord, and some Bible students understand one of the two witnesses in Revelation 11:3–6 to be Elijah, because the rains cease.

The prophecy of Malachi ends with God speaking these words: "See, I will send you the prophet Elijah before that great and dreadful day of the LORD comes. He will turn the hearts of the fathers to their children, and the hearts of the children to their fathers; or else I will come and strike the land with a curse" (Mal. 4:5–6).

The Jews expected that before the Messiah came, Elijah would appear to prepare His way. The angel Gabriel told John the Baptist's father, Zechariah, that his son John would bring the people of Israel back to God by going before the Lord "in the spirit and power of Elijah" (Luke 1:17). Gabriel ended his announcement by quoting the words of Malachi 4:6a. When Zechariah could speak again, he predicted that John would "be called a prophet of the Most High; for you will go on before the Lord to prepare the way for him" (Luke 1:76). The phrase "prepare the way" is also found in Isaiah 40:3.

John the Baptist modeled himself after the prophet Elijah, although he did not believe himself to be Elijah (John 1:21). His dress was similar to Elijah's (Mark 1:6), his home was the desert (Luke 1:80), his preaching was powerfully direct (Matt. 3:7–12;

Luke 3:7–17), and he predicted a judgment of fire (vv. 9, 16–17). Like Elijah, his stand for truth brought him into conflict with rulers (Mark 1:14; 6:17–18). Jesus said that John had fulfilled Malachi's prophecy about Elijah (Matt. 17:10–13).

Neither Elijah nor John the Baptist saw himself as doing anything novel. Rather, they were pointing the way *back* to God by calling people to obey God's commands. There are times when God has to speak forcefully and threaten judgment; these two prophets were in that mold. Both men experienced discouragement in their ministry (see 1 Kings 19:14; Matt. 11:2–3). Neither prophet saw a nationwide revival in Israel even though they were faithful to the call.

One insight we gain from Elijah and John is that God fulfills prophecy precisely, but creatively. John is like Elijah yet different. Instead of calling down fire from heaven, he baptized sinners who sought to be right with God. He preached law but also provided grace. Another insight is the importance of knowing history. Only by knowing about Elijah could anyone recognize that John the Baptist was ministering "in the spirit and power of Elijah." Often today's believers miss what God is doing because they haven't learned Bible history. A final insight about these two prophets is that they reveal the price of taking God's side. Both were perceived as rebels by the ruling power, each suffered for obeying God, and John the Baptist was martyred.

ė See: John the Baptist, Zechariah

ELIZABETH

The reign of King Herod brought dark and difficult days to Judea, but if any woman in Jerusalem at that time had reason to be joyful, it was Elizabeth, the wife of Zechariah the priest (Luke 1:5–23, 39–80). To begin with, she had been born into the nation of Israel, the only nation chosen by the Lord and enjoying a special covenant relationship with Him (see Rom. 9:1–5).

It was through Israel that God promised to bless the whole world by sending the Redeemer (Gen. 12:1–3), and Elizabeth would play an important part in that drama. Her name means "God of the oath," and the God of Israel would indeed keep His promises to Abraham and his people.

Elizabeth could also rejoice because she was married to a priest and could devote her life and home wholly to the service of God. Both of them were descendants of Aaron, Israel's first high priest (Luke 1:5), and her name, Elizabeth, was taken from Elisheba, the name of Aaron's wife (Exod. 6:23). The law of Moses required priests to marry virgins from their own tribe so that the priesthood would not be defiled (Lev. 21:7, 13–15). Zechariah and Elizabeth were people of godly character and obedient to the Lord in every area of their lives.

But there was one shadow over their marriage: Elizabeth was barren, and God had not answered their repeated prayers for children. Now both Zechariah and Elizabeth were very old and, like Abraham and Sarah centuries before (Genesis 15; 18:1–15; 21), they were beyond the time of having children. God gave them a long life, but it must have been a lonely life without children to raise for the Lord. You would think that God would especially bless a godly praying couple like Zechariah and Elizabeth—and He did, in His own time. Their prayers were not forgotten.

It is estimated that there were some eighteen thousand priests available for the temple ministry in that day. They were divided into twenty-four "courses" and each course served two weeks out of the year. The high priest cast lots to see which priest would perform what ministry, and by the providence of God, Zechariah was chosen to burn incense in the holy place on the golden altar that stood before the veil. "The lot is cast into the lap, but its every decision is from the LORD" (Prov. 16:33). Burning the incense was the closest the priests came to the Holy of Holies, except for the high priest who entered that sacred place only on the annual Day of Atonement.

The angel Gabriel, who would later visit Mary, appeared to Zechariah and told him that Elizabeth would bear him a son!

The aged priest was frightened, his faith was weak, and God had to discipline him by making him unable to hear or to speak (see Luke 1:18–20). Imagine Elizabeth's surprise when her husband came home and could only make signs to her or write on a wax tablet. How excited she must have been when she discovered she would give birth to a son who would prepare the way for the ministry of Messiah! As He did with Abraham and Sarah, God "gave life to the dead" (Rom. 4:16–25), and Zechariah knew his wife and she conceived their son (Luke 1:24). Zechariah had to remain silent in a silent world, but he and Elizabeth rejoiced at the precious gift that God was sending them. After all, their son would be the forerunner and herald of the Messiah!

Why did Elizabeth "remain in seclusion" for five months after becoming pregnant? Certainly Elizabeth wasn't ashamed of being pregnant, for the Jewish people considered children the best blessing of God, and she rejoiced that she was no longer barren. In small communities, news gets out and spreads quickly, so the neighbors must have discovered her condition; but it seems they didn't understand its full import until the baby was named (vv. 57–66). The combination of aged Elizabeth's pregnancy and her husband's inability to hear and speak must have aroused a great deal of curiosity, and the couple didn't want to become the center of attention. Their best option was to remain at home as much as possible and prepare for their son's birth. After all, if the forerunner is about to be born, the Messiah can't be far behind!

Six months after Elizabeth became pregnant, Gabriel visited Mary in Nazareth and announced that she would become the mother of the promised Messiah (vv. 26–38). He gave her a special word of encouragement when he said, "Even Elizabeth your relative is going to have a child in her old age, and she who was said to be barren is in her sixth month. For nothing is impossible with God" (vv. 36–37). Mary believed the words of the angel and hurried to visit her relative "in the hill country of Judea."

How could Elizabeth and Mary be related when Elizabeth descended from Aaron, the first high priest, and Mary from the family of David (Luke 3:31)? Aaron had been married prior to being called to priestly ministry and his wife Elisheba came from the tribe of Judah (Exod. 6:23; Num. 2:3–4). You will find Nashon and Amminadab mentioned in Mary's genealogy (Luke 3:32–33). It's interesting that Aaron's marriage united "king" and "priest" and prefigured the ministry of Jesus Christ as the King-Priest "after the order of Melchizedek" (see Heb. 5:10; 7:1–28). Melchizedek was the king-priest of Salem in the days of Abraham (Gen. 14:18–20) and is a type of Jesus Christ in His present heavenly ministry as King and Priest (Heb. 7:1–3).

When Elizabeth heard Mary's voice, the babe in her womb leaped for joy, and Elizabeth was filled with the Spirit and began to praise God. Note that she said to Mary, "Blessed are you among women" (Luke 1:42) and not "above women." She also said, "Blessed is she who has believed" (v. 45), because it was Mary's faith in God's promise that was commendable. Zechariah had doubted God's promise and been silenced, but Mary believed the Word and broke out in song.

In her hymn of praise, Elizabeth magnified Mary's Child, the Son of God. Mary's presence was a blessing and a privilege, primarily because of the Child she would bear. The unborn John leaped for joy at the voice of Mary because she was the "mother of [the] Lord." Elizabeth commended Mary for her faith in the Word of the Lord and for what the Lord had accomplished and would yet accomplish. The two mothers-to-be spent three months together (v. 56), and since Zechariah wasn't able to hear or speak, Mary's presence in the home was a special help to Elizabeth. Mary remained there until John was born, although she isn't mentioned in the birth narrative. When you remember that Zechariah and Elizabeth were elderly people and that Mary was probably fifteen or sixteen, you realize how wonderful it is that faith in the Lord brings people together and unites them in heart. If we are walking in the Spirit, there are no generation gaps.

❦ See: John the Baptist, Mary, Zechariah

EPIPHANY

The word *epiphany* means "revealing" or "revelation." The early Christians considered the coming of the Magi to worship the Christ Child (Matthew 2) as a fulfillment of Isaiah 60:1–3—"Arise, shine, for your light has come, and the glory of the LORD rises upon you. See, darkness covers the earth and thick darkness is over the peoples, but the LORD rises upon you and his glory appears over you. Nations will come to your light, and kings to the brightness of your dawn." Jesus was a Jew, but the salvation He brought was for all peoples. Jesus was and is "a light for revelation to the Gentiles and for glory to your [God's] people Israel" (Luke 2:32).

Epiphany was established by the third century, before any official celebration of the nativity. The birth of Christ, the coming of the shepherds, the adoration of the Magi, and the Lord's baptism were all originally connected to the January 6 festival. Eventually, in Western Christendom, Epiphany focused on the Magi worshiping the newborn King, and in the East the focus was on the Lord's baptism. By highlighting the truth that Jesus is the world's Savior and that Gentiles are saved through faith in Jesus, the Church declared its mission to take the gospel to the world.

Once December 25 was established as the Feast of the Nativity, the Christmas season filled the days until Epiphany (January 6), creating the twelve days of Christmas (start counting with the day after Christmas).

❧ See: Christmas, Gifts, Wise Men, Xmas, Yuletide

FAITH

Every person lives by faith. Someone may deny it saying, "I don't believe in God or ghosts or life after death!" Nevertheless, each of us utilizes faith in some way. For instance, if we see the doctor who orders a prescription, we take the medicine, believing the pharmacist has followed the doctor's orders. When we take our car on the road, we trust that the other drivers are going to follow the rules of the road and not hit us. We go to work and do our best, believing that we will be paid on time. Every day we exercise faith.

The word *believe* is used twice in Luke 1 (*believe* is the verb form of the noun *faith*). First, Gabriel told Zechariah he would be unable to speak until his son was born because he "did not believe" (v. 20). Second, when Mary reached Elizabeth's house to visit, Elizabeth proclaimed, "Blessed is she who has believed what the Lord has said" (v. 45). Zechariah and Mary each had an opportunity to respond to God in faith. His failure to believe cost Zechariah his speaking privileges for just over nine months. Mary's submissive act of faith brought glory to God, salvation to sinners, and honor to her.

– F –

What distinguishes faith in God from faith in the pharmacist? Why do we wrestle with God's will for our lives but we drive into expressway traffic without a worry? Using Zechariah and Mary as examples, let's explore this experience of faith in God.

Faith focuses on promises, not explanations. In response to the news that he would be a father, Zechariah asked, "*How* can I be sure of this?" (v. 18). He was convinced that he and his wife were too old and he missed Gabriel's words about this being an answer to prayer (v. 13). Instead of rejoicing in the good news, he wanted details about the process. His lack of faith rendered him silent.

Mary posed a similar question to Gabriel when he visited her: "How will this be, since I am a virgin?" (v. 34). This question was not born of doubt, but rather of concern for purity. Mary was engaged to Joseph, she knew where babies came from, and she knew marriage should come before having children. Gabriel did in fact explain the process by which she would become pregnant: the Holy Spirit would "overshadow" her (v. 35).

There is more to reality than we can see, feel, or think. Therefore our limitations don't limit God, who is infinitely original. Sometimes faith must go beyond reason. An older couple having a child is unusual but not impossible (think of Abraham and Sarah). Zechariah believed that being old eliminated him and Elizabeth from becoming parents—that was the "reasonable" approach. In the end, he was glad to be wrong.

Mary believed God could cause her to conceive in her womb apart from sexual activity and that God could convince those who needed to know the truth. She heard Gabriel's words about the identity of her son and about the activity of the Holy Spirit and she responded with faith: "I am the Lord's servant. May it be to me as you have said" (v. 38). And it was.

Faith rests on the character of God. After Gabriel told Mary about the Spirit's overshadowing and that her relative Elizabeth was pregnant in her old age, he proclaimed, "Nothing is impossible with God" (v. 37).

Mary knew who God is and what He is like. Her Magnificat (vv. 46–55) exalts the attributes and activity of the God she trusted, powerfully expressing Mary's deep faith. But faith is only as good as its object. Because she knew God's character, she took Him at His word. So Elizabeth greeted Mary saying, "Blessed is she who has believed that what the Lord has said to her will be accomplished!" (v. 45).

Zechariah focused on the "how" and lost sight of "Who" was speaking to him. During his enforced silence, Zechariah's faith bloomed again and was beautifully communicated in his Benedictus (vv. 67–79). Faith requires the right content, and Zechariah's song majestically celebrates who God is and what He does.

Faith sees the risks but focuses on the rewards. Mary knew her pregnancy would raise questions and invite gossip. She also knew that the Lord was with her, that her Child would be the promised Messiah, and that nothing was impossible with God. Mary submitted to God's plan. Trusting Him, she faced the heart-wrenching difficulties with Joseph and her family, she endured the comments and looks from the villagers, and she withstood the charge that Jesus was illegitimate. When she held the promised Child in her arms, she felt joy because God had kept His promise.

People of faith don't expect trusting God to make life un-complicated or convenient. God has unusual ways of shaping our lives and getting us to where He wants us to be. He doesn't tell us ahead of time what He's doing. He wants us to rest in His hands, enjoy the adventure, and be surprised by what He accomplishes.

Faith is vindicated by God's action. It took time, but eventually Gabriel's words to Zechariah came true (v. 20). Zechariah didn't believe Gabriel when they spoke in the temple, but once Elizabeth became pregnant, how could he deny it? John the Baptist was born, grew up, and prepared the way for the Lord.

Mary and Joseph traveled to Bethlehem, where Jesus was born. Then they were forced to travel to Egypt to avoid Herod's murderous rage. Finally they returned to the Holy Land and settled in Nazareth. At age twelve, Jesus demonstrated his awareness of being God's Son (2:41–52). At about thirty, He was baptized and began His public ministry as the Messiah. Three and a half years later, He was crucified. He rose again. All the promises made by God were fulfilled in Jesus' life, death, and resurrection. Mary was right to believe in God.

"Faith is being sure of what we hope for and certain of what we do not see" (Heb. 11:1).

꙾ See: Elizabeth, God, Mary, Prophecy, Songs, Zechariah

"FEAR NOT"

In the King James Version of the Bible, the phrase "fear not" is found three times in Luke's Christmas narrative and four additional times in his Gospel. The New International Version translates it, "Do not be afraid." The author of this Gospel was a physician—Paul called him "our dear friend Luke, the doctor" (Col. 4:14)—and often doctors have to say to their patients, "Now, don't be afraid." No wonder Luke used the phrase seven times in his Gospel!

Fear was a great problem at the time Jesus came into the world. According to Matthew 4:16—a quotation from Isaiah 9:2—the people were "living in darkness . . . in the land of the shadow of death." Death was a terrible enemy that kept many people in bondage to fear (Heb. 2:14–15), and the pagan religions had no answers or assurances to offer. People lived in spiritual darkness and longed for light. It was not until Jesus "destroyed death and . . . brought life and immortality to light through the gospel" (2 Tim. 1:10) that the darkness fled and the fear of death vanished for those who believed. When you examine the occasions when an angel or the Lord Jesus Himself said "Do not be afraid," you will better understand why Christian believers need never fear.

God Answers Prayer (Luke 1:11–25)

The aged priest Zechariah was burning incense in the holy place of the temple in Jerusalem when suddenly the angel Gabriel appeared at the side of the golden altar that stood before the veil. It was such a surprise that the old man was startled and frightened. Had he done something wrong? Was the Lord going to slay him? "Do not be afraid, Zechariah," the angel said to him, "your prayer has been heard" (v. 13). Throughout their married life, Zechariah and his wife, Elizabeth, had been praying for a son, but none had been given. Now they could be sure that the son they longed for would be born to them, and not just any son, but the promised forerunner of the Messiah (Mal. 3:1; Luke 1:76). Are you frightened about a situation, a disappointment, a delay in God's working? Don't be afraid— God still answers prayer.

God Gives Us Grace (Luke 1:26–38)

Six months later Gabriel came to Nazareth and appeared to Mary, the devoted young virgin God had chosen to be the human channel through whom His Son would come into the world. The angel's sudden appearance and his greeting greatly troubled Mary. How was she "highly favored"? How would the Lord be "with her" and why? Gabriel calmed her heart by saying, "Do not be afraid, Mary, you have found favor with God" (v. 30). The word translated "favor" is the Greek word for "grace." A literal translation of the angel's words would be, "Grace to you who are highly graced! You have found grace with God!"

Mary was not called to an easy task, for she would be misunderstood and would endure much personal sorrow (2:34–35). But God's grace would always be available and adequate. The word translated "highly favored" in Luke 1:28 is applied to all believers in Ephesians 1:6 and translated "his glorious grace, which he has freely given us in the One he loves." God's abundant grace is available to us just as it was to Mary! Why should we be afraid?

God Has Good News for Us (Luke 2:8–20)

The work of the shepherds in the fields was pretty much routine. They had to keep watch for predators that might attack the flocks, and there was always the danger of sheep wandering away. But for the most part, the work was uneventful. Perhaps the men were discussing the sad plight of Israel, suffering under the iron heel of the Roman emperor and King Herod. David's throne was empty and the long-awaited Messiah had not appeared. Imagine the fear the shepherds experienced when the glory of the Lord illumined those familiar fields and an angel spoke to them! "Do not be afraid. I bring you good news of great joy that will be for all the people" (v. 10). What was the good news? The promised Savior had been born! The choir of angels from heaven praised God and then all was silent again. The shepherds wasted no time going to Bethlehem to see this Child and then they spread the good news far and wide.

In the darkest night, when circumstances seem at their worst, God sends His messengers with good news. That messenger probably won't be an angel from heaven. He or she might be a neighbor from up the street, a preacher you hear over the radio, a friend from church, or a total stranger. There is always good news when we keep our eyes of faith open to God's Word. When you read your Bible, don't see it as a collection of stories, threats, or laws, but as a series of promises, the good news that God is for us and wants us to succeed for His glory.

There are four remaining "fear not" statements in Luke.

God Is Greater than Our Sins (Luke 5:1–11)

When Peter saw the miracle Jesus performed—the huge catch of fish—he felt so overwhelmed and unworthy that he almost wrecked his future ministry by wanting to abandon his call to discipleship. But Jesus said to him, "Don't be afraid; from now on you will catch men" (v. 10). Think of what a tragedy it would have been if he had missed the very best Jesus had planned for him! Yes, we are unworthy of the least of God's blessings, and yet He gave us His very best, His Son. Let's not look at ourselves; let's keep looking to Jesus (Heb. 12:1–2).

God Is in Control (Luke 8:40–56)

Jesus was willing to go to the home of Jairus to heal his dying daughter, but a woman delayed Jesus; and while He was helping her, news came that the little girl had died. Our Lord said to the distraught father, "Don't be afraid; just believe, and she will be healed" (v. 50). Our Lord always has everything in His control, even when there are disappointments and delays. His timing is never wrong.

God Considers Us Precious (Luke 12:7)

Jesus was encouraging His disciples not to fear the threats of people or circumstances. If the Father cares for the little sparrows, surely He will care for His own children. "Don't be afraid; you are worth more than many sparrows."

God Secures the Future (Luke 12:32)

"Do not be afraid, little flock, for your Father has been pleased to give you the kingdom." The Father doesn't give us just a crown or a throne; He gives us the kingdom! The future is not a question mark; it's an exclamation point! No matter what our trials may be now in this life, we will one day be with the Lord and reign with Him.

🍃 See: Joseph, Mary, Shepherds, Zechariah

FIRSTBORN

Luke 2:7—Mary "gave birth to her firstborn, a son"—is the first of six verses in the New Testament that apply to Jesus the remarkable title "firstborn." In Jewish family life, the firstborn son was special and received twice as much inheritance from his father as did the other sons (Deut. 21:15–17). "Firstborn" was a title of honor and rank and did not always reflect birth order. Israel was God's "firstborn" among all the nations that preceded her (Exod. 4:22). David was the eighth son in Jesse's family (1 Sam. 16:10–13), but God made him His "firstborn" (Ps. 89:27). "Firstborn" implies priority and superiority, the very highest of the high. This is why it is applied to Jesus Christ.

The Firstborn over All Creation (Col. 1:15)

Jesus is not a created being; He is the eternal Son of God, the Creator of everything. "Through him all things were made; without him nothing was made that has been made" (John 1:3). Paul's letter to the Colossian believers emphasizes "that in everything he [Jesus] might have the supremacy" (Col. 1:18), and that applies to believers individually and to the churches to which they belong.

Is it any wonder that this marvelous planet on which we live has gradually been selfishly exploited and wastefully destroyed, when the world has left the Creator out of its plans and purposes? In matters of ecology and stewardship, Jesus Christ is no longer supreme; He is ignored and even defied. Christmas reminds us that Jesus is the Lord of the universe and that we must obey Him if we intend to enjoy and employ His creation for our good and His glory. He is the firstborn—the Supreme One—over all creation.

The Firstborn from among the Dead
(Col. 1:18; Rev. 1:5)

The resurrection of Jesus Christ is the seventh such miracle recorded in the Bible, but it is the greatest of them all. The three dead persons raised in the Old Testament (1 Kings 17:22; 2 Kings 4:34–35; 13:20–21) and the three raised in the Gospels (Luke 7:14–15; 8:52–56; John 11:38–44) all came forth with bodies still subject to death, and they died again. But Jesus came forth with a glorified body that could never die again. He lives and ministers in heaven by the "power of an indestructible life" (Heb. 7:16).

How can birth and death be combined in one phrase—"firstborn from among the dead"? Paul answers that question in Acts 13:32–33—"We tell you the good news: What God promised our fathers he has fulfilled for us, their children, by raising up Jesus. As it is written in the second Psalm: 'You are my Son; today I have become your Father.'" This is a quotation from Psalm 2:7 and refers to the resurrection of Jesus Christ and not to His birth. The tomb into which the body of Jesus was placed became as it were a "womb" out of which He was "born" into a new life with a glorified human body. He is the highest and the greatest of all who have been or who will be raised from the dead, and one day all believers will be like Him (Phil. 3:20–21; 1 John 3:1–3).

The Firstborn among Many Brothers (Rom. 8:29)

On resurrection morning, Jesus said to Mary Magdalene, "Go . . . to my brothers and tell them, 'I am returning to my Father and your Father, to my God and your God" (John 20:17). Hebrews 12:23 calls the family of God "the church of the firstborn." This means that God's people hold the highest position and will receive a full inheritance from the Father. Imagine every child in the family, male and female, receiving the inheritance of the firstborn!

One of the obvious facts in Scripture is that God rejects the firstborn (and our first birth) and accepts the second-born (and our second birth). He rejected Cain and chose Abel and then Seth (Genesis 4); He rejected Ishmael and chose Isaac (16; 21:8–21); He rejected Esau and chose Jacob (25:19–34). God slew the firstborn in Egypt, for by our first birth we are condemned (Exodus 12). Those who trust Jesus Christ are born again, and this "new birth" brings salvation (John 3).

Jesus the "Firstborn" Deserves Worship (Heb. 1:6)

"And again, when God brings his firstborn into the world, he says, 'Let all God's angels worship him.'" This is a quotation from Deuteronomy 32:43 in the Greek version of the Old Testament. Some students apply this verse to the birth of Jesus at Bethlehem, for the angels did praise Him when He was born (Luke 2), while others emphasize the word "again" in the verse and apply it to His second coming. What a contrast between His first coming and His second coming! He was born in poverty, obscurity, and weakness but He will return in power and great glory and defeat His enemies (Rev. 19:11–21). At His first coming, He brought salvation; but when He comes again, He will judge and condemn those who have rejected the truth. His "firstborn family" will live and reign with Him forever. It is a privilege to be a child of God in the "church of the firstborn," and we ought to live and serve as those who appreciate that privilege.

❧ See: Immanuel, Jesus, Messiah, Nazarene

GENEALOGY

Genealogies make us think about roots. Every family tree has its heroes and villains. Knowing where you came from, and who is in your family tree, helps to shape your identity and experience.

For a king to claim his throne, he must prove that he is descended from the royal bloodline. The two New Testament genealogies trace Jesus' family connection to King David. Matthew 1:1–17 provides Joseph's family tree, beginning with Abraham and ending with Jesus. Luke 3:23–38 traces Mary's lineage, beginning with Jesus and going back to Adam. Both genealogies affirm that Jesus is a true descendant of King David and therefore Jesus can rightly lay claim to David's throne. Together they identify Jesus as a descendant of Abraham (and therefore a Jew, Matt. 1:1–2; Luke 3:33) and as a descendant of Adam (and therefore human, v. 37).

Some persons get frustrated by all those difficult-to-pronounce names in the genealogies, wondering why they're included in Scripture. The names tell us, first of all, that God is a God of individuals: each person is important to God. In fact God knows each of us by name (Isa. 43:1; John 10:3). Second, each person in the genealogies had a part in God's plan to bring the Savior to earth. Each generation brought the Messiah's arrival closer. Third, every family has members who are trophies of God's grace, like Jacob, Tamar, Rahab, Ruth, and Bathsheba ("Uriah's wife"), as listed in Matthew.

Many families have recorded their family tree in the family Bible. It's an efficient way of keeping track of all the relatives. When you see your own name, you realize it's good to belong to the family. But most important, it's good to belong to God's family. Do you?

◊ See: David, Elizabeth, Joseph, King, Messiah, Prophecy

GIFTS

God is a constant giver. He gives us life, health, food, family, resources, ability, work and rest, day and night, sun and rain, seasons, friends, guidance, answered prayer, grace and peace and joy. God's greatest gift to us is Himself, in the person of Jesus Christ who is God the Son.

Unwrapping a gift is part of the joy of receiving it. What waits beneath the covering? Special gifts require special gift wrap. Koreans practice the art of *pojagi*, which includes wrapping special gifts with brightly colored and carefully patterned textiles that delight the eye and hand. A *pojagi* wrapping cloth means the gift is significant and that the giver intends great good for the recipient. The wrapping is as important as the gift itself.

When God gave His Son to the human race, He wrapped Him perfectly—in a body! "When Christ came into the world, he said: 'Sacrifice and offering you did not desire, but a body you prepared for me'" (Heb. 10:5). "The Word became flesh" (John 1:14). God the Son in human flesh is unique, fully God and fully human. *The* Christmas gift is Jesus. God gave His infinite, eternal Son to sinners. In Jesus, God gives eternal life.

In giving us Jesus, God gave everything that we need spiritually. Ponder the words of Galatians 4:4–7:

> But when the time had fully come, God sent his Son, born of a woman, born under law, to redeem those under law, that we might receive the full rights of sons. Because you are sons, God sent the Spirit of his Son into our hearts, the Spirit who calls out, "Abba, Father." So you are no longer a slave, but a son; and since you are a son, God has made you also an heir.

St. Paul is telling us that, when we receive Jesus, we receive additional gifts from God. These include the gift of spiritual freedom, the gift of a spiritual family, the gift of the Holy Spirit, and the gift of our spiritual inheritance. These are blessings we enjoy because of Jesus' birth, life, death, and resurrection. At Christmas, God gave us a gift that does not wear out or lose its value or grow boring. The better we know Him, the richer a treasure Jesus is.

When we give gifts to others at Christmas, we are imitating God. Of course those who don't know God do it unconsciously. God's giving was intentional, and our giving should be as well. Let's dare to probe this practice of giving gifts.

A good starting point is *why we give*. What are our motives? Giving should be a joy, not a burden. When we give because it's tradition or because it's required, it can get to be a seasonal expense that we resent. Giving to get produces neither joy nor satisfaction. Some persons give gifts to impress others. But the best reasons to give a gift are still love and to meet a need. God gave us Jesus because He loves us (John 3:16; 1 John 4:9–10). By giving us Jesus, God met our deepest need: to be forgiven of sin and to have life after death.

Another consideration about gift giving is *how we give*, and the wise men who brought gifts to Jesus provide a worthy example. Their gifts were appropriate for a king, and they gave according to their means (going into debt to give Christmas gifts is not good stewardship). Their gifts were planned long before they found the Child. The wise men offered their gifts joyfully, and their gifts blessed Mary and Joseph as well as baby Jesus (Matt. 2:9–11).

When we actually present the gift, we should do so thoughtfully, deciding ahead of time what we will say to the person as we place the gift in his or her hands. "Here, this is for you!" isn't as meaningful as "I believe this gift reflects a part of your sparkling personality. I hope you enjoy it." Good presentation matters in gift giving (the art of *pojagi*).

Most gift tags have two words: "To" and "From." What if we changed the second word to "Because"? Then the tag might read, "To my wife" "Because of Jesus." Or "To my son" "Because God loves you." This creates an opportunity to make the spiritual motive for the gift crystal clear.

Here is an observation about *what we give*. Our gift reveals how well we know the recipient. A thoughtful gift will take into consideration his or her tastes, needs, experiences, and circumstances. Some folks like gifts that provide an experience (dining out, a trip, or skydiving), while others prefer material objects (a book, fountain pen, or clothing).

Since we will probably get some gifts at Christmas, we should contemplate *how we receive* a gift. Our relationship with the giver is more important than the gift itself. We should appreciate the thought, effort, and cost that went into the gift. Our attitude should be humble and we should be ready to be surprised. After we've opened the gift, our words and gestures should express gratitude. What if it's a gift you don't want? Be grateful anyway! (Try not to be one of those relatives who announces immediately that he's going to exchange the gift.)

One aspect of gift giving remains to be explored: *what we give to God*. Obviously God needs nothing. Yet it delights the heart of God when His children offer their gifts. Over the course of Advent and Christmastide, and throughout the year, these gifts are appropriate:

- Time—alone with God, to listen and to pray, to simply enjoy God's presence

- Love—telling God why you love Him and doing acts of service for others to demonstrate your love
- Obedience—to God's Word, in all areas of life, without arguing
- Praise—in silence, with spoken word, in song
- Worship—privately but especially in God's house with God's people
- Giving—practicing biblical stewardship
- Thanksgiving—list on paper the ways God blessed you today
- Trust—submit to God's plan and timing

Perhaps poet Christina Rossetti phrased it best in the carol we know as "In the Bleak Midwinter."

> What can I give him, poor as I am?
> If I were a shepherd, I would bring a lamb;
> if I were a Wise Man, I would do my part;
> yet what I can I give him: give my heart.

❧ See: Grace, Immanuel, Wise Men, Word

GLORY

From the human point of view, glory means achievement, fame, and publicity, with perhaps authority and money thrown in; but when we speak of "the glory of God," it means something far different. "All men are like grass, and all their glory is like the flowers of the field. . . . The grass withers and the flowers fall, but the word of our God stands forever" (Isa. 40:6, 8). Everything God is and does is glorious, and His glory never changes. Human glory is like fireworks that dazzle us for a few seconds and then vanish, but God's glory is like the sun that is always radiant. Clouds may hide it but they cannot put it out. Therefore, the Lord is worthy of all praise and honor, for nothing in all creation excels the magnificence of the Lord. He alone is worthy of praise and worship, and our greatest privilege is to worship "the glorious Father" (Eph. 1:17) and the Son who glorifies the Father (John 5:23). "So whether you eat or drink or whatever you do, do it all for the glory of God" (1 Cor. 10:31; see Matt. 5:16).

The Jewish people were privileged to have God's glory abiding with them, for "theirs [is] the divine glory" (Rom. 9:4). When Moses dedicated the tabernacle, God's glory moved in (Exod. 40:34–35; Lev. 9:22–24); but when Israel repeatedly rebelled against God, the glory departed (1 Sam. 4:21). Solomon dedicated the temple to the Lord, and once more the glory filled the edifice (2 Chron. 7:1–3), and the people fell on their faces to worship God. But again the nation and its leaders repeatedly sinned, and the glory departed (Ezek. 9:3; 10:4, 18–19; 11:22).

The glory of God returned to earth when Jesus was born at Bethlehem. "The Word became flesh and made his dwelling among us. We have seen his glory, the glory of the One and Only, who came from the Father, full of grace and truth" (John 1:14). The Savior laid aside His eternal glory that He might come to earth as a servant (17:5), and He glorified the Father in His ministry on earth (v. 1). He received that glory back when He returned to the Father in heaven (v. 5), and one day all believers will see that glory and share in it (v. 24). All of God's children have that glory within them today (v. 22), and one day that glory will be revealed for all to see (Rom. 8:21–25, 29–30).

"The heavens declare the glory of God" (Ps. 19:1). This was certainly true when the star appeared to the wise men and led them to Bethlehem. The shepherds saw God's glory when the angels appeared to them in the fields and they heard the angels praise God for His glory. The experience so moved them that they glorified God in the witness they gave to others (Luke 2:9, 14, 20).

Where is God's glory today? It is still reflected in His creation, but it also dwells in each individual believer (1 Cor. 10:31), in each faithful local church (1 Cor. 3:16–17—the pronouns are plural), and in the universal Church made up of all who have trusted Christ (Eph. 1:22; 2:19–22; 3:20–21). When we glorify God in our lives and in corporate worship, the unsaved are convicted and want to believe in Jesus and be saved. "But if an unbeliever or someone who does not understand comes in while everybody is prophesying, he will be convinced by all that he is a sinner and will be judged by all, and the secrets of his heart will be laid bare. So he will fall down and worship God, exclaiming, 'God is really among you!'" (1 Cor. 14:24–25).

God created us to share His glory, not only in this life but throughout eternity. We lost that glory because of sin (Rom. 1:21–23; 3:23), and it can be restored only through personal faith in Jesus Christ (Rom. 5:1–2).

> Hark! the herald angels sing,
> "Glory to the newborn King!"
> Charles Wesley

❦ See: Angels, Nazarene

GOD

God reveals His perfect character in all that He says and all that He does, and this is especially true in the Christmas narrative. When you read carefully Matthew 1–2 and Luke 1–2, you discover the greatness of Almighty God.

A Triune God

In Luke 1:30–35 the angel Gabriel calmed Mary's fears by assuring her that God looked in favor (grace) on her. Then Gabriel explained that she would be the vessel God would use to bring His Son into the world. Mary didn't doubt these words but she did wonder how they would be accomplished in the body of an unmarried virgin. Gabriel explained that this would be the work of the Holy Spirit. So here we have the Triune God—the

Father and the Son and the Holy Spirit—working together to accomplish the miracle of the virgin birth. (See also Matthew 1:18–23.) The doctrine of the Trinity is basic to the Christian faith. The text of our Lord's sermon at Nazareth emphasized the Trinity (Luke 4:18–19), and so did His discourse in the upper room (John 14:15–21, 26; 15:26; 16:5–16). The apostle Paul taught this doctrine often in his epistles (Rom. 1:1–7; 8:9–11, 26–27; 15:16; 2 Cor. 1:20–22; 13:14; Gal. 4:4–6; Eph. 1:3–14; 3:14–19; 2 Thess. 2:13–14; Titus 3:4–6). A famous theologian once said, "Try to explain the Trinity and you may lose your mind. Explain it away and you will lose your soul."

A God of Great Power

"For nothing is impossible with God" (Luke 1:37). The angel Gabriel knew what he was talking about, for he had seen the Lord create the universe by merely speaking the word (Job 38:4–7) and he knew about every miracle recorded in the Old Testament. In the 1901 American Standard Version, Luke 1:37 reads, "For no word from God shall be void of power." The psalmist made it clear: "For he spoke, and it came to be; he commanded, and it stood firm" (Ps. 33:9). Only God can speak the word and the night sky will blaze with His glory and a remarkable star will guide travelers from the East. Only God can cause His eternal Son to become a human baby, without sacrificing His deity, and be born from Mary's womb. "Is anything too hard for the LORD?" (Gen. 18:14).

A God of Great Love

"For God so loved the world that he gave his one and only Son, that whoever believes in him shall not perish but have eternal life" (John 3:16). This familiar verse reminds us that Jesus did not come to condemn the world but to save all who would believe in Him. "And we have seen and testify that the Father has sent his Son to be the Savior of the world" (1 John 4:14). "But God demonstrates his own love for us in this: While we were still sinners, Christ died for us" (Rom. 5:8). Because of their great love, the Father gave the Son and the Son gave His life. "This is how God showed his love among us: He sent his one and only Son into the world that we might live through him" (1 John 4:9).

A Faithful God

Speaking about Jesus, the angel Gabriel said, "The Lord God will give him the throne of his father David, and he will reign over the house of David forever; his kingdom will never end" (Luke 1:32–33). Mary sang, "He has helped his servant Israel, remembering to be merciful to Abraham and his descendants forever, even as he said to our fathers" (vv. 54–55). Filled with the Spirit, Zechariah the priest said, "Praise be to the Lord, the God of Israel, because he has come and has redeemed his people . . . (as he said through his holy prophets of long ago)" (vv. 68, 70). God made covenant promises to His people and He kept every one of them. At the close of a long life, Joshua said to the people of Israel, "You know with all your heart and soul that not one of all the good promises the LORD your God gave you has failed. Every promise has been fulfilled; not one has failed" (Josh. 23:14). King David sang, "O Sovereign LORD, you are God! Your words are trustworthy, and you have promised these good things to your servant" (2 Sam. 7:28). The Christmas narrative reminds us that God can be trusted. He remembers His holy covenant and He keeps His promises (Luke 1:68–79).

A God Who Answers Prayer

All their married life, Zechariah and Elizabeth had prayed for a son and had joined the faithful Jewish remnant in asking God to send the promised Redeemer. Year after year, it seemed that God wasn't listening, but then the angel told Zechariah that his prayer had been heard (Luke 1:13). Only a God of love is willing to hear His people's prayers; only a God of wisdom knows how to answer; only a God of power can provide that answer. We can only marvel at the providence of God as He brought everything together at the manger in Bethlehem.

A God Who Responds to Faith

Because Mary believed God's promise (Luke 1:45), she was blessed and rejoiced at the fulfillment of His Word. "I am the Lord's servant," she said. "May it be to me as you have said" (v. 38). Because Zechariah doubted God's promise, he became silent and deaf until eight days after his son was born. When we trust ourselves, we get whatever we can do, but when we trust God, we get what only God can do. "Some trust in chariots and some in horses, but we trust in the name of the LORD our God" (Ps. 20:7). No wonder Paul prayed, "May the God of hope fill you with all joy and peace as you trust in him, so that you may overflow with hope by the power of the Holy Spirit" (Rom. 15:13). Note those five monosyllables—"as you trust in him."

God of Glory

Whatever God does will ultimately lead to His glory. "The LORD will give grace and glory" (Ps. 84:11 NKJV). Paul combines these words in Ephesians 1:6—"to the praise of his glorious grace." The Christmas narrative is filled with the glory of God. The shepherds beheld "the glory of the Lord" around them (Luke 2:9), and the angels praised God's glory because of His favor to mankind (v. 14). The shepherds glorified God by sharing the good news God had told them (v. 20). Old Simeon sang in the temple, "For my eyes have seen your salvation, which you have prepared in the sight of all people, a light for revelation to the Gentiles and for glory to your people Israel" (vv. 30–32).

During the Christmas season, some people complain about the gifts they receive and say, "I surely deserve more than this!" They have forgotten about God's grace, because none of us really deserves anything! And yet the Father has given us His very best and most costly gift—His one and only Son (John 3:16).

We could mention many more attributes of God found in Matthew 1–2 and Luke 1–2 but we will give you the joy of discovering them for yourself. As you celebrate the birth of Jesus Christ and read, hear, and sing the Christmas story, be alert to identify the attributes of God and then praise God for His greatness.

❦ See: Gifts, Glory, Grace, Love

GRACE

God in His grace gives us what we don't deserve, and God in His mercy doesn't give us what we do deserve—judgment. God's grace is possible because of what Jesus accomplished on the cross. The word *grace* is often translated "favor" in modern versions of the New Testament, because favor is something that sinners can't earn and don't deserve. That God chose Mary to bear Jesus was an act of grace (Luke 1:28—literally "Joy to you who are highly graced"). In her song The Magnificat (vv. 46–55), Mary took none of the credit and gave all the glory to God.

While they were growing up, both Jesus and John the Baptist experienced the grace of God (Luke 1:80; 2:40, 52). In Titus 2:11–14 and 2 Corinthians 8:9, Paul emphasized God's grace in the coming of Jesus to earth to be our Savior.

Someone made a helpful acrostic of the familiar word *grace*:

God's
Resources
Available to
Christians
Everywhere

Grace comes from God, for He is "the God of all grace" (1 Pet. 5:10). His resources of grace are so vast that Paul wrote about "the riches of his grace" (Eph. 1:7; 2:7). These riches are available to all of God's children in every circumstance of life. It's not our performance or our perfection that determines God's generosity, but only His abounding grace. This doesn't mean we should use grace as an excuse to sin (Rom. 6:1–4; Jude 4), nor should we become so legalistic that we "set aside the grace of God" or "[fall] away from grace" (Gal. 2:21; 5:4). We are saved by grace (Eph. 2:8–9) and we must live by grace (1 Cor. 15:10).

The best "Christmas text" about grace is 2 Corinthians 8:9—"For you know the grace of our Lord Jesus Christ, that though he was rich, yet for your sakes he became poor, so that you through his poverty might become rich." Jesus was rich in heaven, yet He laid it all aside and became poor on earth so that He might make rich all who believe in Him. The verb indicates "once and for all" action and refers to the incarnation. Paul described this wonder in Philippians 2:1–11, and it is illustrated in John 13:1–17, when Jesus washed His disciples' feet.

The church at Laodicea thought it was rich when it was really poor (Rev. 3:17–18), while the church at Smyrna thought it was poor but was really rich (2:9). "For in Christ all the fullness of the Deity lives in bodily form, and you have been given fullness in Christ" (Col. 2:9–10). Not emptiness but fullness! God's people may not have great material riches that fade away or can be stolen but they do have spiritual riches that never fade away and that nobody can steal (Matt. 6:19–34), and they have God's promise that He will meet their every need (Phil. 4:19). Paul described himself as "poor, yet making many rich; having nothing, yet possessing everything" (2 Cor. 6:10). What a paradox—and what a privilege!

The word *grace* isn't used widely in Christmas songs but it hasn't been completely overlooked. The second verse of Charles Wesley's "Come, Thou Long-Expected Jesus" reads—

> Born Thy people to deliver,
> Born a child and yet a King.
> Born to reign in us forever,
> Now Thy gracious kingdom bring.

"Joy to the World" by Isaac Watts has "grace" in the last verse—"He rules the world with truth and grace." The beloved "Silent Night" by Joseph Mohr says in verse three:

> Silent night, holy night,
> Son of God, love's pure light;
> Radiant beams from Thy holy face
> With the dawn of redeeming grace,
> Jesus, Lord, at Thy birth,
> Jesus, Lord, at Thy birth.

In verse one of "It Came upon the Midnight Clear" by Edmund H. Sears, you find, "Peace on the earth, good will to men, from heaven's all-gracious King."

For the most part, the world doesn't understand the meaning of grace. Most people think we earn our way into heaven by our good works and that God saves the righteous. But there are no righteous, "for all have sinned and fall short of the glory of God" (Rom. 3:23). "I have not come to call the righteous, but sinners to repentance," said Jesus (Luke 5:32). He couldn't call the righteous people because there aren't any! "There is no one righteous, not even one" (Rom. 3:10). That's the reason all of us must depend wholly on the grace of God.

♪ See: Songs

GREETINGS

A greeting is intended to acknowledge someone's presence, get his or her attention, and engage the person in conversation. However, the words we use to greet others during Advent and Christmas have become the subject of hostile debate. Political correctness demands that "Merry Christmas!" be replaced by "Season's Greetings!" or "Happy Holidays!"

For followers of Jesus Christ, the Advent/Christmas season is about Jesus; therefore, "Merry Christmas!" best communicates both our faith and our reason for rejoicing (*merry* means "festive, filled with joy and laughter"). Within the family of faith, "Merry Christmas!" is always appropriate. In the wider world, we must boldly express our faith in Christ but we might want to consider some alternative expressions.

The most common greeting given to the main characters of Advent and Christmas was "Do not be afraid" (see "Fear Not"). This was how Gabriel spoke to Zechariah (Luke 1:13) and to Mary (v. 30) and how an angel addressed both Joseph (Matt. 1:20) and the shepherds (Luke 2:10). But there were other phrases used as well. Gabriel said to Mary, "The Lord is with you" (1:28). The angels announced to the shepherds "good news" (2:10).

Ponder what could happen if Christians began to greet others with alternative biblical phrases. What might people think, and how might they respond, to a reassuring "Fear not!"? What kind of questions might come in response to "Good news!"? What internal defenses might crumble if someone heard, "The Lord is with you!"?

Christmas greetings are required for the season. Choose your words thoughtfully.

& See: Angels, "Fear Not," Mary, Shepherds, Zechariah

HEROD THE GREAT

Herod the Great is the only Herod who figures in the birth of Christ. He founded the Herodian dynasty, and John the Baptist and Jesus each had to deal with members of that family. In the biblical record, Herod the Great appears in Matthew 2:1–19 and Luke 1:5.

Herod began his career as a military man but pushed his way to the top in politics. First he governed Galilee, added Syria, and finally was made King of Judea by Augustus (37 BC). He was not a Jew but an Idumean (Edomite). His ruthless leadership style perpetuated a triangle of conflict between himself, Jewish leaders, and Caesar.

Herod did not follow the Jewish religion personally and never let it influence him politically. He deprived the Sanhedrin of its civil power, relegating its members to a religious role. Josephus reports that Herod built a theater in Jerusalem and held games there every five years. His subjects disliked him but they feared him. Rebuilding the temple in Jerusalem was his greatest architectural achievement. As he neared the end of his life, his anger grew uncontrollable, and to spite the Jews, Herod erected a golden eagle at the temple gate—an act interpreted as sacrilege and insult.

Because he could not discern the truth from lies and gossip, Herod was not loyal to family or friends. He was responsible for the deaths of a wife, a mother-in-law, two brothers-in-law, and three sons. Josephus characterized Herod in these words: "A man he was of great barbarity toward all men equally" and "a slave to his passions."

It is not surprising that Herod felt threatened by the Magi's inquiry, "Where is He who has been born King of the Jews?" (Matt. 2:2 NASB). Herod thought he was king of the Jews and he did not tolerate opposition, even from a child. His interaction with the Magi conveys the sense of an actor manipulating his audience, using them to identify his rival. Herod was an angry old man when Jesus was born. The cold-blooded murders of the baby boys under age two in Bethlehem is consistent with what we know of Herod's character and conduct.

Herod's response to Jesus set the pattern for how rulers and governments have often dealt with Jesus and His followers. A Christian's highest loyalty is to Christ, and some states perceive that as a threat. This explains the persecution of Christians in nations that ignore human and religious rights. The state is often focused on control; Jesus brings freedom.

The tragedy and grief in Bethlehem is a dark shadow in the Christmas story. We wish it had not happened. Indeed, we wish no child would die! Evil produces terror and pain and sorrow. Joseph was told in a dream to take Mary and Jesus to Egypt, and they were saved. Other infants died and their parents were devastated with horror and grief. Those babies died so Jesus could live. People still die today because of Jesus.

↯ See: Bethlehem, Egypt, Innocents

HOLY SPIRIT

The true "spirit of Christmas" is the Holy Spirit, the third Person of the Trinity, without whom there could have been no

Christmas. The Spirit inspired the Old Testament prophecy of Messiah's birth (Isa. 7:14) as well as the New Testament fulfillment (Matt. 1:18, 20). "The Holy Spirit will come upon you," the angel Gabriel told Mary, "and the power of the Most High will overshadow you" (Luke 1:35). It was a miracle nobody can fully explain.

But the Spirit brought blessings to others besides Mary. He filled John the Baptist from birth and equipped him for his ministry (v. 15). He filled Elizabeth with blessing when she heard Mary's greeting (v. 41), and He filled Zechariah the priest and enabled him to speak and hear again and to deliver a prophecy (vv. 67–79). The Spirit was upon aged Simeon and told him he would not die before he had seen the promised Messiah. The Spirit led him to Mary and Joseph and Jesus in the temple and put within his heart and upon his lips a song of praise to the Lord as well as a prophecy concerning Jesus and Mary (2:25–35).

We must also remember that the Holy Spirit inspired the prophet Micah to write the prophecy that led the wise men from Jerusalem to Bethlehem (Mic. 5:2; Matt. 2:1–12).

Love, joy, and *peace* are words often used during the Christmas season, and this is what we desire for everyone; but those blessings can come only through the Holy Spirit. "But the fruit of the Spirit is love, joy, peace" (Gal. 5:22). However, we can't receive these wonderful blessings of the Spirit unless we first receive the gift of Jesus Christ the Savior. "But when the time had fully come, God sent his Son, born of a woman, born under law, to redeem those under law, that we might receive the full rights of sons" (4:4–5). That's the *Christmas event.* Paul tells us who came, when He came, how He came, why He came. But knowing these historical facts doesn't save us. We must turn from our sins, believe God's promise, and ask Jesus to save us. Then we shall have the *Christmas experience!* "Because you are sons, God sent the Spirit of his Son into our hearts, the Spirit who calls out, '*Abba*, Father'" (v. 6). Trusting Jesus means you receive the true Christmas Spirit!

The Christmas event happened but once, at Bethlehem, when Jesus Christ was born into this world, but the Christmas experience is repeated over and over as sinners turn by faith to Jesus and call on Him for salvation. Jesus called this experience being "born again" (see John 3:1–16). It means making a new beginning, receiving a new life, and having your sins forgiven.

The Christmas event with friends and family is a very special time, but the enjoyment doesn't last. People try to recapture a distant childhood Christmas and rekindle a dead fire, but it doesn't work. For God's people, the Christmas experience is ever fresh and joyful because the Holy Spirit makes Jesus real to us through His Word. This kind of experience brings blessings that last forever.

Have you had this experience?

𝆑 See: Hope, Immanuel, Overshadow, Virgin Birth

HOPE

In the years before Christ's birth, there was a growing sense of hopelessness among the peoples of the world. Many people felt that the old religions had failed, but there was nothing to make them believe that better days were coming.

The people of Israel had hope—they anticipated the coming of their promised Messiah. Simeon was waiting for "the consolation of Israel" (Luke 2:25), the arrival of Israel's Redeemer and King. The prophet Isaiah offered hope in these words:

> The people who walk in darkness will see a great light; those who live in a dark land, the light will shine on them. . . . For a child will be born to us, a son will be given to us; and the government will rest on His shoulders; and His name will be called Wonderful Counselor, Mighty God, Eternal Father, Prince of Peace.
>
> *Isaiah 9:2, 6 NASB*

The promised child, a son, would shine light into Israel's darkness by being the perfect Ruler. Godly people hoped and prayed for His speedy arrival.

The New Testament uses the word *hope* more than eighty times—it is a book of hope! God's gift of salvation through Jesus Christ provided hope not only for Israel but for all the Gentile peoples as well (Rom. 15:12). God is "the God of hope" (v. 13). The birth of God's Son means hope for every person alive today.

Let's ask some questions as we investigate Christian (and Christmas) hope.

Who Needs Hope?

People who have heard the doctor say, "There's nothing more we can do," need hope. The athlete who didn't make the team needs hope, as do the victims of injustice and violence, the man who lost his job, the grieving mother, the teenager tired of the daily grind, those with tearstained cheeks and a sin-sick soul, families whose loved ones serve in the military, the person who no longer finds a purpose in life, sinners who cannot escape the power and guilt of their sin. Who needs hope? We all do! The whole world needs hope.

What Is Hope?

Some skeptics belittled those with hope. H. L. Mencken defined hope as "a pathological belief in the occurrence of the impossible." Benjamin Franklin said, "He who lives on hope will die fasting."

Hope is not optimism based on positive circumstances. Hope is the ability to believe in the good when things are bad. "Hope means hoping when things are hopeless or it is no virtue at all. It is only when things are hopeless that hope begins to be a strength" (G. K. Chesterton). Hope is an undefeated forward look.

Christian hope is facing the present reality with confidence in future good because of God's action in Jesus Christ. Hope is living now, knowing that God is preparing something better. Hope expects God to take what's painful and mysterious and turn it ultimately into eternal good (see Rom. 8:24–25). Hope also prevents us from getting comfortable when all is well.

What Do We Hope For?

We hope for peace. We hope for a world without war, terrorism, child abuse, divorce, and nuclear threat. We hope for answers to our questions that start with Why . . . ? We hope for an end to suffering. We hope for change: change in ourselves, in others, our circumstances, our attitudes, and our conduct. We hope for sufficient resources to meet all of life's challenges. We hope for success in what we do in working, parenting, witnessing, and being a friend. We hope for friends we can trust and life that has meaning. We hope for heaven.

Where Can We Find Hope?

Hope is rooted in a person, Jesus Christ. Paul began his first letter to Timothy by calling Christ Jesus "our hope" (1:1). Jesus is the enduring source of Christian (and Christmas) hope. His death for sin and His resurrection give us absolute confidence to face the future, including death. Christians grieve when a loved one dies, but we grieve with hope (1 Thess. 4:13). Because our relationship to Jesus is secure, we will ultimately experience everything that God has prepared for His people. This is why a personal relationship with Jesus Christ is essential. Have you experienced the hope that only Jesus gives?

The gospel is another place we can find hope. The "hope held out in the gospel" (Col. 1:23) includes the reality that our sin is forgiven and we are not what we used to be. The gospel proclaims that God is making us to be like His Son (Rom. 8:29). Peter wrote that we have received "new birth into a living hope" (1 Pet. 1:3), meaning that the Christian life moves toward a glorious future, despite life's difficulties. Salvation will be a finished work when we stand before the Lord (Phil. 1:6). The presence of Christ dwelling in us now is our "hope of glory" (Col. 1:27). Our hopefulness should be a reason unbelievers ask about our faith in Christ (1 Pet. 3:15).

Our hope needs to be nurtured by the truth of God's Word: "For everything that was written in the past was written to teach us, so that through endurance and the encouragement of the Scriptures we might have hope" (Rom. 15:4). Stories of the saints motivate us to carry on. Think of Noah, Abraham, Sarah, Moses, Esther, Jeremiah, the Virgin Mary, and John the Baptist.

God's promises found in Scripture also nourish our hope. The promises provide strength to endure (v. 4). This tells us that true Christian hope is capable of waiting. The experiences of Bible saints teach us that God always, ultimately, responds to hopeful waiting. "Let us hold unswervingly to the hope we profess, for he who promised is faithful" (Heb. 10:23). What promise do you need to claim to bolster your hope? Here is a short list of Advent and Christmas promises of what Jesus can do for us:

- "The government shall be on his shoulders" (Isa. 9:6).
- "He will be their peace" (Mic. 5:5).
- "He will save his people from their sins" (Matt. 1:21).
- "They will call him Immanuel—which means, 'God with us'" (Matt. 1:23).
- "A Savior has been born to you; he is Christ the Lord" (Luke 2:11).
- "The Word became flesh . . . full of grace and truth" (John 1:14).
- "He tends his flock like a shepherd: he gathers the lambs in his arms and carries them close to his heart; he gently leads those that have young" (Isa. 40:11).
- We have "the light of the knowledge of the glory of God in the face of Christ" (2 Cor. 4:6).
- "The Son of God appeared . . . to destroy the devil's work" (1 John 3:8).

- "This is how God showed his love among us: He sent his one and only Son into the world that we might live through him" (1 John 4:9).

God the Holy Spirit also sustains our hope: "May the God of hope fill you with all joy and peace as you trust in him, so that you may overflow with hope by the power of the Holy Spirit" (Rom. 15:13). The Holy Spirit does not let us focus on what is wrong or painful. He consistently points us to Jesus, who is our source of hope. The Spirit works to reproduce the character of Jesus in us, genuinely transforming us. The hope provided by the Spirit is not a trickle, but a constant stream, so that we "overflow with hope." That doesn't mean we ignore life's realities or turn a blind eye to serious issues. It means having an undefeated forward look because the Holy Spirit is present and at work in us.

Christ's return is another source of the believer's hope. Jesus promised He would return and take us to be with Him (John 14:3). When he appears, "we shall be like him, for we shall see him as he is. Everyone who has this hope in him purifies him-self" (1 John 3:2–3). Our hope of Christ's return will motivate holy living so we're ready to welcome Him. His return means peace and justice and joy and heaven. The reality will exceed our anticipation!

Are You a Hopeful Person?

The old saying is, "Where there's life, there's hope." That's wrong! We should say, "Where there's hope, there's life!" When your hope is anchored in Jesus, you are truly alive.

Ponder these evidences of being a hopeful person: giving to God's work even when the economy is shaky, investing in missions during wartime, continuing to serve even if you're not appreciated, expressing love despite being treated unkindly, praying and witnessing even when the results are slow in coming, facing death by anticipating heaven. Hopeful people know

God is at work and God is trustworthy. They expect that the way things are is not the way things will stay.

Christian (and Christmas) hope means living in the future tense.

❧ **See: Anna, Baby, Bethlehem, Simeon**

i

IMMANUEL

This name of Jesus means "God with us" and is found in Isaiah 7:14 and 8:8, 10, as well as in Matthew 1:23. There is no record in the New Testament that anybody other than the angel ever associated this name with Jesus, but the meaning of the name—the presence of Jesus with His people—is seen throughout the Bible. "And surely I am with you always, to the very end of the age" (28:20). This is not a promise with conditions attached; it is the statement of a wonderful fact. Whether we realize it or not, He is with us.

First, a bit of ancient history. The name Immanuel was revealed to the prophet Isaiah seven centuries before Jesus was born (see Isaiah 7). King Ahaz and the kingdom of Judah were in deep trouble because the powerful Assyrian empire was threatening to swallow up the small kingdoms of Judah, Israel (the northern Jewish kingdom), and Syria. Israel and Syria wanted Ahaz to join them in an alliance against Assyria, but Ahaz refused. He had secretly made a treaty with Assyria that the other kings knew nothing about (2 Kings 16:5–9), so he couldn't very well turn against his ally. Instead of trusting the Lord to deliver

Judah, he was relying on the Assyrians, who were actually his enemies.

When you read Isaiah 7, you meet a frightened king, a trembling nation, and a confident prophet. Isaiah told the king that the only sure way to have peace was to trust in the Lord and not in political alliances. He promised that God would defeat the enemy kings and rescue Judah, and he even offered to give Ahaz a sign from the Lord to strengthen his faith. Hypocritical Ahaz piously refused the sign, so Isaiah gave the sign to the entire house of David to which Ahaz belonged. This was the sign: a woman, then a virgin, would be married and conceive a child and name him Immanuel—"God with us." Before the child would reach the age of accountability—to the Jews, twelve years old—the two enemy kings would be dead and the northern kingdom of Israel would be taken by Assyria. Isaiah delivered this prophecy in 734 BC and in 732 Assyria defeated Syria and in 722 invaded the northern kingdom and absorbed it into its empire. But Judah was delivered; Isaiah's words from the Lord proved true.

There's more to the name Immanuel than an assurance that God's Word is true. The name teaches us important truths about Jesus Christ and the way He cares for His people.

To begin with, it teaches us that Jesus is both God and man, divine and human. Isaiah didn't write that a "man of God" or a "godly man" would be with us but the God-Man, the Son of God Himself in sinless human flesh. *Jesus Christ is God!* (see John 1:1, 14; 20:28; Rom. 9:5; Titus 2:13; Heb. 1:8; 2 Pet. 1:1; 1 John 5:20). He claimed to be God (John 10:30–33; 14:1–9; 19:7) and He received worship as God (Matt. 2:11; 14:33; John 9:38). He took on Himself sinless human nature so that He could reveal the Father to us (John 14:1–9). He entered into our everyday human experiences so He could become our sympathetic High Priest (Heb. 2:9–18; 4:14–16; 5:7–10). He surrendered His body on the cross as a sacrifice for our sins so that we might receive eternal life (10:1–14; 1 Pet. 2:24).

Theologians call this "the incarnation," from two Latin words that together mean "in the flesh, in a body." Jesus, who existed from eternity in heaven, willingly emptied Himself of His own independent use of His divine attributes and came to earth as a servant (Phil. 2:1–11). What condescension! This was not a temporary "embodiment" for one specific task, as in the Old Testament appearances of Jesus (Genesis 18; 32; Josh. 5:13–15; Daniel 3), but a permanent union of His divine nature with human nature. Empowered by the Holy Spirit, Jesus did the Father's will day after day. Today He is glorified in heaven, and one day all believers shall be like Him (1 John 3:1–3).

While ministering here on earth in that prepared human body (Heb. 10:5–7; Ps. 40:6–8), Jesus was limited by time and space as was any other human. If He was in Capernaum, He was not in Bethany. But the exalted King-Priest in heaven today is unlimited. *He is with each of His people constantly and available to them to meet their needs.* When we serve Him, He is working with us (Mark 16:20). When we are in difficult places, He is with us to assist us (Acts 18:9–11; 23:11; 27:19–25; 2 Tim. 4:16–18).

Even in the hour of death, He is with us (Ps. 23:4), and He will be with us for all eternity (Rev. 21:1–3). Jesus has promised, "Never will I leave you; never will I forsake you" (Matt. 28:19–20).

Charles Spurgeon said it beautifully. "'God'—there lies the majesty. 'God with us'—there lies the mercy. 'God'—therein is glory. 'God with us' is grace."[1]

Majesty—mercy—glory—grace! Immanuel—God with us!

ê See: Gifts, Jesus, Messiah, Nazarene

INCARNATION

Incarnation comes from two Latin words that mean "in the flesh, in a body." Incarnation is the theological term used to express the doctrine that Jesus Christ is God in a human body. "The Word became flesh" (John 1:14). Jesus is both fully God

---

1. Charles Spurgeon, *Metropolitan Tabernacle Pulpit* (Pasadena, TX: Pilgrim, 1980), 21:711.

and fully human, one person, but with two natures. For a more thorough discussion, see Advent and Immanuel.

❧ See: Advent (Christ's First), Prophecy, Virgin Birth

INN

The story of Mary in labor and Joseph desperately seeking shelter and the innkeeper refusing them a room because his establishment was full, is dramatic—and probably fiction.

Today's travelers expect to make a reservation at a motel and have a room waiting when they arrive. Almost every exit on America's highways has at least one facility for overnight guests. It was not this way in the ancient world.

Travelers journeyed in caravans and camped for the night. There were inns along the main business routes but they were not nice places. Most were just a level camping area by an oasis, but some were enclosed facilities, with two stories. The accommodations were poor, the company not the best, and innkeepers had a bad reputation. Theft was common, and it was dangerous to be alone.

Bethlehem did not have this type of inn because it was too far off the main caravan routes. It was a busy town when Joseph and Mary arrived due to all the individuals and families there to register for the census (Luke 2:1–3). Most out-of-town guests would have stayed with relatives, but even that kind of housing probably filled up quickly.

Luke tells us that while Joseph and Mary were in Bethlehem, the time came for her to deliver her child. The idea that Mary was in labor when they arrived in town is probably wrong; it was after they had arrived that her labor began.

The word for "inn" (κατάλυμα, *katalyma*, in Luke 2:7) would be better translated "guest room." The word is never used for a public guest facility in the Arabic and Syriac versions of Luke's Gospel. "No room for them in the inn" would be interpreted to mean that "the guest room" was full at a relative's house.

Most houses at the time had an upper and lower level. The lower level was where the family's animals were kept. Sometimes this lower level was divided, so the family could sleep on one side and animals could stay on the other. Animals would be fed at a manger (made of wood or stone).

If there was no room available in the main part of the house for Mary and Joseph to sleep, they could have gone to the lower-level sleeping quarters. And this is where Mary gave birth to Jesus. Then the manger, which was nearby, would have made a convenient cradle (Luke 2:7).

Among the Christmas legends are stories of the animals speaking or singing for baby Jesus. The fanciful accounts point at least to the fact that Christ was born where animals were kept. By the time the Magi arrived (Matthew 2), Joseph and Mary and baby Jesus were living in a house. So the "barn" was only temporary quarters.

The circumstances of Jesus' birth reveal that Joseph and Mary were poor and needed to rely on the kindness of others. Where Jesus was born indicates how crowded Bethlehem was and how difficult it must have been to find a private place for Jesus' birth. It may not have been what Mary and Joseph wanted or expected, but God did provide a safe, warm place for Jesus to be born. God always meets our needs.

è See: Bethlehem, Christmas, Manger, Mary, Shepherds

INNOCENTS

December 28 on the Church calendar commemorates the Slaughter of the Innocents, Herod's brutal murder of baby boys to rid himself of the threat of another (genuine) King of the Jews (Matt. 2:1–18). That Herod was threatened by an infant and that he perpetrated such violence reveal that he was a mean man ruled by fear and anger. His attempt to use the Magi to discover the newborn King's location was malicious. He wanted the information only so that he could commit murder. When his quarry escaped, he committed murder anyway.

Imagine that you are one of the fathers or mothers whose boy is not yet two years old. You hear the tramp of soldiers' feet come down your street. There's a knock on the door. A soldier demands to know if there are young children, boys. Soldiers search the house. Despite tears and struggle, the little ones are seized—and killed. For the devastated parents, it means shock, horror, anger, and grief. As we read the story, we feel those same emotions.

Matthew reached back to words of the prophet Jeremiah to express the feeling in Bethlehem: "A voice is heard in Ramah, weeping and great mourning, Rachel weeping for her children and refusing to be comforted, because they are no more" (Matt. 2:18; Jer. 31:15). The kind of grief that cannot be comforted—that's what the families in Bethlehem knew.

During Advent and at Christmas, we want the illusion that all is well. The truth is, Christmas sharpens the knife-edge of our own sorrows and problems. Bethlehem was the place of the divine mystery of the incarnation. It was also a place of human brutality. This is a difficult topic to address. But let us meditate on some of the ways this scriptural account touches us.

The death of the innocents breaks our hearts. We ache for the little ones and for their parents and siblings. Bethlehem was not a large town, and some scholars estimate there were perhaps a dozen or twenty baby boys. But if one child dies, that's too many! If twenty baby boys died, that's forty bereaved parents. Daily we see the effects of war on children and we hear reports of children abused or missing or dead. One healthy response is to cry, like Rachel. We can also seek to comfort those who mourn. Whose broken heart might God use you to heal?

The death of the innocents opens our eyes. Evil is real, embodied in human beings. Herod was evil—murder was nothing new to him. Evil persons are selfish, proud, and opposed to

God. Herod tried to destroy Jesus and he ended up destroying himself.

Behind human opposition to Christ is Satan. Satan hates that Jesus is honored, loved, and obeyed, so he strikes at the followers of Jesus. One reason Jesus came to earth was to destroy the works of the devil (1 John 3:8). The devil has been defeated by Christ's death and resurrection but he still fights. Where do you see evil at work? Are you willing to overcome evil with good? Will you be loyal to Jesus if Christians are accused of being "the enemy"?

The death of the innocents troubles our minds. This account provokes questions that have no satisfying answers: Why did God let innocent children die? Why did He let those parents suffer? Why did the soldiers obey such an immoral order?

To the question, Why doesn't God protect the innocent? the answer is: *we* should protect the innocent! But sometimes evil wins, despite our best efforts.

What happens to children who die before they can understand who Jesus is and what He did for them? Here are four biblical considerations. First, when King David's infant son died, David said, "I will go to him, but he will not return to me" (2 Sam 12:23). David believed that he would see his child again in heaven. Second, Christ's sacrifice on the cross was sufficient for all persons. Third, God is gracious. Fourth, Jesus loves children. "He took the children in his arms, put his hands on them and blessed them" (Mark 10:16). While it is never explicitly spelled out in Scripture, God through Christ's death and resurrection has made provision for those who are too young to respond to the gospel.

The death of the innocents exercises our faith. Logical thinking and good theology won't heal the wounds and grief inflicted by evil. Surviving is a matter of having faith in the living God. Remember that Christmas led to Calvary. The innocent Son of God experienced injustice, evil, and murder.

Isaiah 63:9 offers a gift of words to those in mourning: "In all their affliction He was afflicted" (NASB). These words give us reasons to believe: God is with us in our afflictions. God knows how it feels to be afflicted. God will carry us through our afflictions. How do we know? Jesus was afflicted to death—and He is alive forever.

🕯 **See: Herod the Great, Wise Men**

JESUS

Choosing a child's name is both a privilege and a responsibility. Many parents begin the selection process when they know a child is in the womb. Nearly all parents have names ready by the time labor pains begin, although there have been circumstances when a child wasn't named until some weeks after being born (perhaps the mother and father disagreed about a name).

Mary, however, knew from the moment she said yes to God that she would have a son and that she was to name Him Jesus (Luke 1:31). Joseph received the same command: "You are to give him the name Jesus, because he will save his people from their sins" (Matt. 1:21). Perhaps this was one of the ways God convinced Joseph that Mary's pregnancy was a divine act, in that they were both told to name the child Jesus.

In Bible times, names were more than what you called a person. A name had meaning. It indicated a person's character and perhaps his or her purpose in life. *Jesus* is the Greek form of the Hebrew name Joshua (Yeshua), and it means "Jehovah saves" or "God is salvation." The angel told Joseph to name the child Jesus because Jesus would save His people from their sins (v. 21). The eighth day after His birth, He was formally given the name Jesus at His circumcision (Luke 2:21).

God's Son was given the human name Jesus because the human race has a fundamental problem: sin. Sin is not simply a passive inability to meet God's standards. Sin is our active, intentional rebellion against God, His commands, and purposes. Sin is in our nature, and sins are what we do wrong. Every sin is an offense against a holy God. The consequences of sin are God's wrath and our death.

God's Son was named Jesus because He came to solve our problem with sin. Sin is *our* problem, but His mission was to save us from sin. He did that by living a sinless life, willingly dying in our place on the cross, and rising again to never-ending life. When a person "receives" Jesus as Savior (John 1:12), he or she is forgiven of sin and is given eternal life (3:16). Only Jesus can save us from our sins and give eternal life, because only He is sinless, and therefore only He is qualified to be the sacrifice for our sin. Further, only Jesus conquered death by rising from the grave. Jesus is God's sole sufficient solution to the problem of our sin.

Because only Jesus can save us from sin, we need a relationship with Him. How should we think of this relationship? What should it look like? Our relationship to Jesus the Savior begins when we understand that He is a gift to receive. "Yet to all who received him, to those who believed in his name, he gave the right to become children of God" (1:12). When we receive Jesus—believe in Him at the heart level—He enters our lives, and His presence includes the gift of salvation. There is no way to earn forgiveness. There is no possibility of our being good enough to deserve salvation. Jesus' birth, life, death, and resurrection are acts of God's grace. Only by receiving the gift of Jesus are we forgiven, rightly related to God, and certain of eternal life. Once you have a relationship with Jesus, you can't live without Him. Have you received Jesus?

Our Leader

As our relationship with the Savior grows, we discover that He is a leader to follow. When Jesus called His disciples, He often commanded "Follow Me!" (Mark 1:17, 2:14; John 1:43 NASB). A follower follows. That is, a true follower of Jesus understands that Jesus leads the way and that He doesn't need our suggestions on where to go or how to get there. In Bible times when a rabbi chose a disciple, the disciple's task was to imitate the rabbi, learn from him, and as much as possible become like the leader. Is Jesus your leader? Do you trust Him? Are you a good follower?

Our Master

Because Jesus is our Savior, He must be the master we serve. Often the disciples referred to Jesus as Master (Luke 5:5; 8:24, 45; 9:33, 49), and Jesus told parables featuring masters and servants (Matt. 13:24–30; 18:21–35; 22:1–14; Luke 19:12–26). The master is in charge. His servants do not argue with his commands; they obey. Jesus Himself was a servant, so He understands perfectly the servant's role: "For even the Son of Man did not come to be served, but to serve" (Mark 10:45). Jesus expects loyalty from His servants ("no one can serve two masters"—Matt. 6:24). He taught His servants that they would be treated like their Master, meaning we will suffer (John 15:18–25). He emphasized that no servant is greater than his master (13:16; 15:20). He encouraged His servants by promising, "Where I am, my servant will also be. My Father will honor the one who serves me" (12:26). What kind of servant are you?

Our Friend

As our Savior, Jesus is also a friend to embrace. In life we have many acquaintances but few real friends. Jesus said, "You are my friends if you do what I command. I no longer call you servants, because a servant does not know his master's business.

Instead, I have called you friends, for everything that I learned from my Father I have made known to you" (John 15:14–15). Servants know what to do; friends know why they're doing it. Jesus lets us into His thoughts and plans, although He doesn't explain everything. Jesus is the friend who sticks closer than a brother (Prov. 18:24) and He is the friend of sinners (Luke 7:34). Does Jesus call you "friend"?

Our King

Perhaps the highest privilege of knowing Jesus the Savior is worshiping Him as King. Both Isaiah and Micah prophesied that Messiah would be a king (Isa. 9:6–7; Mic. 5:2–5a) and at His birth the Magi came to Jerusalem asking, "Where is the one who has been born king of the Jews?" (Matt. 2:2). On His cross was a sign stating, "THIS IS JESUS, THE KING OF THE JEWS" (Matt. 27:37). Because of His servant's life and obedient death, "God exalted him to the highest place and gave him the name that is above every name, that at the name of Jesus every knee should bow, in heaven and on earth and under the earth, and every tongue confess that Jesus Christ is Lord, to the glory of God the Father" (Phil. 2:9–11). Jesus is absolutely sovereign. Unlike earthly kings, Jesus uses His position and authority to bless and serve His people. The proper posture before a king is to kneel, submitting to his lordship. Do you willingly bend the knee to King Jesus?

Jesus Is God

Often in Scripture, and in conversation, our Savior is referred to as Jesus Christ. Those are not His first and last names. *Jesus* is His human name, reminding us that God is our salvation. *Christ* is the Greek word for anointed One or Messiah. So the two names together express that Jesus is God, come to save us by fulfilling the prophesied work of the Messiah.

"Give him the name Jesus" (Luke 1:31). "You are to give him

the name Jesus, because he will save his people from their sins" (Matt. 1:21). Jesus is the greatest name in heaven and earth!

è See: David, Grace, Immanuel, Joseph, King, Mary, Messiah, Nazarene

JOHN THE BAPTIST

Most of the season of Advent centers on the infant Jesus. The person of John the Baptist forces us to make a leap forward in time, to when Jesus is an adult. This may seem like an anachronism but it is not. At Christ's birth, the world was prepared culturally and politically. But before the Messiah could accomplish His work of salvation, Israel had to be prepared spiritually. This was the mission of John the Baptist, and Advent is a fitting time to emphasize his work.

John the Baptizer is a "saint" of the Advent season. Each year he appears in the Gospel readings on the second and third Sundays of Advent. We learn about his background, we hear snatches of his preaching, and we know he demanded repentance. John baptized publicly those who confessed their sins (Matt. 3:6; Mark 1:4; Luke 3:3). This was unusual—and attention getting—because the Jews did not practice baptism (only Gentiles who converted to Judaism experienced a kind of washing). John the Baptist takes the stage briefly during Advent and then disappears. We need to know more about this colorful figure!

John's mission in life was to point to Jesus. He was a witness to the light (John 1:7–8). From events before his birth to the circumstances of his death, John's life was shaped by his relationship to Jesus. This should be true for every person who is a follower of Jesus.

John grew up knowing the story of the angel Gabriel's conversation with his father in the temple (Luke 1:5–25). He knew that his birth was against the odds, his parents being well on in years, and he knew that his name had been given by the angel

(v. 13). From his earliest days John realized that he was chosen for a special role in God's program—he was to be the forerunner to the Messiah (vv. 17, 76). As John learned the Scriptures for himself, he understood that certain passages applied specifically to him (Isa. 40:3–5; Mal. 4:5–6). After reaching adulthood, John chose to live in the desert (Luke 1:80). Like the prophet Elijah, John the Baptist seemed to appear out of nowhere when his public ministry began.

Since Mary and Elizabeth were relatives (v. 36), some Bible scholars speculate that Jesus and John were cousins (second? third?). John was older than Jesus by several months, and perhaps they saw each other occasionally as they grew up. It seems that John did not know Jesus was the Messiah until he baptized Jesus (John 1:31). John treated Jesus with the highest respect, acknowledging he wasn't worthy to untie Jesus' sandals, and insisting Jesus was the greater person (Matt. 3:11; Mark 1:7–8; Luke 3:16; John 1:26–27, 33).

Luke introduces John to his readers with beautiful irony:

> In the fifteenth year of the reign of Tiberius Caesar—when Pontius Pilate was governor of Judea, Herod tetrarch of Galilee, his brother Philip tetrarch of Iturea and Traconitis, and Lysanias tetrarch of Abilene—during the high priesthood of Annas and Caiaphas, the word of God came to John son of Zechariah in the desert.
>
> *Luke 3:1–2*

Luke listed all the significant politicians. Then he named the priests. We might expect God to speak to and through these important leaders. But to Luke they were merely background figures. The "word of God" came to John because the real power—God's—was at work in John, the last of the old covenant prophets, divinely appointed forerunner to the Messiah, who was fulfilling ancient prophecy and serving in the spirit and power of Elijah (1:17). The peoples of Palestine thought Caesar, Herod, or the high priest held the real power. God bypassed the high and mighty and sent His word to John.

Instead of locating near the centers of religious and political power, John did his preaching and baptizing in the wilderness by the Jordan River (Matt. 3:1; Mark 1:4–5; Luke 3:3). In Mark 1:6 we see that his clothing wasn't the height of fashion (a camel's hair garment and leather belt) and his diet was not gourmet fare (locusts and wild honey). John had a green, organic lifestyle before it became trendy. His environment, lifestyle, and confrontational style of preaching linked him in people's minds to Elijah the prophet (John 1:21).

Preparing Israel to receive her Messiah required John to work on four related tasks at the same time. He called people to repentance, identified Jesus as the Savior, provided evidence that Jesus is the Messiah, and encouraged godly living.

Calling People to Repentance

First, John called people to repentance. Both Matthew (3:1–2, 7–12) and Luke (3:7–18) include portions of John's preaching against sin and spiritual complacency. "Repent" means to change one's mind. The image is that in sin we are moving away from God; when we repent, we turn around and move toward God. We are sorry for our sin and purpose to live a pure life.

Sin alienates us from God, and John drew vivid word pictures to affirm the truth of God's judgment. He spoke of the "coming wrath" (Matt. 3:7; Luke 3:7), a phrase that would have reminded Jews of "the day of the Lord," referenced in their Scriptures (see Isa. 13:9; Joel 1:15; 2:1–2; Amos 5:18–20; Mal. 3:2; 4:1, 5). How many of John's listeners connected him to the predicted coming of Elijah prior to judgment, as found in Malachi 4:5–6?

Another image John used was an ax chopping down a tree (Matt. 3:10; Luke 3:9) and he insisted the ax was *already* at the tree's roots. This meant that God's judgment for sin was currently underway, and those who thought judgment was a long way off were mistaken. Israel's prophets had depicted the nation as a vine planted by God, but her sin would bring destruction (Isa. 5:1–7; Jer. 2:21–22; Hosea 10:1–2). God expects fruit in

His people's lives, and John added the image of unfruitful trees being burned with fire to motivate persons unconcerned about their sin (Matt. 3:10; Luke 3:9). Again, the prophets of Israel had invoked the threat of fire to express God's anger against sin (Jer. 11:16–17; Ezek. 15:6–7).

The winnowing fork and threshing floor images further represented divine judgment in John's preaching (Matt. 3:12; Luke 3:17). A winnowing fork was used to toss the harvested grain into the air. The heavier kernels of grain fell to the threshing floor, and the much lighter chaff blew away on the wind. The grain was stored for use, but the chaff was burned. A person's response to the gospel determined if he or she were wheat or chaff. John's preaching convicted sinners of their guilt, convinced them of God's judgment, and brought them to repentance.

John also challenged the spiritual complacency of his hearers. He warned them against saying, "We have Abraham as our father" (Matt. 3:9; Luke 3:8), as though ethnic identity and religious heritage are what provide us with God's blessing. John stunned his audience by stating that God could make Jews out of rocks, meaning it required God's action to save a sinner, not genetics or traditions.

The Messiah, whose coming John heralded, would divide people into believers who would be saved or unbelievers who would be judged. John confronted people with a spiritual decision; many repented, confessed their sin, and were baptized (Matt. 3:5–6). John preached "a baptism of repentance for the forgiveness of sins" (Luke 3:3). The baptism was not the source of forgiveness; God's forgiveness was the response to repentance and faith. The significance of John's baptism was as an outward expression of an inward spiritual transformation. His preaching was painfully blunt but it expressed "the good news" of salvation (v. 18). John fulfilled his father's prophecy about giving "his people the knowledge of salvation through the forgiveness of their sins" (1:77).

In preaching repentance, John was also fulfilling Isaiah's prophecy (40:3–5, quoted in Matt. 3:3; Mark 1:2–3; Luke 3:4–6).

He also identified himself as the "voice" about whom Isaiah spoke (John 1:22–23). By repenting and being baptized, people were allowing God to rearrange the inner landscape of their lives. As they pursued holiness, God would fill in the eroded places, lower the proud places, and straighten the crooked places in sinners' lives. This is the work God wants to do: make us straight and level.

Identifying Jesus as the Savior

To prepare Israel spiritually for her Messiah, John identified Jesus as the Savior. Zechariah had predicted that John would be a "prophet of the Most High" who would prepare the way of the Lord, so God's people could experience salvation (Luke 1:76–77). Israel expected her long-awaited Messiah to save the nation militarily and politically. John's mission was to bring the people of Israel "back to the Lord their God . . . to turn the hearts of the fathers to their children and the disobedient to the wisdom of the righteous—to make ready a people prepared for the Lord" (vv. 16–17).

Preaching repentance was a prophet's expected work. Baptizing Jews who did repent was new and unprecedented, since it wasn't a Jewish rite. So responding to the gospel at the heart level and being publicly baptized was an act of humility for a son or daughter of Israel. Perhaps it was the pride of the Pharisees in resisting John's message that drew his sermonic attention to them (Matt. 3:7; Luke 7:30). In any event, John knew that he was sent by God to baptize with water as part of his ministry (John 1:33).

John also knew that he was to baptize the Messiah but he didn't know who the Messiah was (vv. 31, 33). So John's baptism had two purposes: (1) a way for repentant sinners to express their inward, spiritual transformation; and (2) a way to identify the Messiah, on whom the Holy Spirit would rest when the Messiah was baptized. This accounts for Jesus' insisting that John baptize Him (Matt. 3:13–15).

Mark's Gospel states that John came "preaching a baptism of repentance for the forgiveness of sins," and that those he baptized confessed their sins (1:4–5). Jesus had no sins to confess or be forgiven. Why, then, was Jesus baptized by John? There are several reasons: to be identified by John as the Messiah (John 1:32–34); to be publicly commissioned in His role as Messiah (the Holy Spirit descended on Jesus like a dove, and the Father pronounced His blessing on the Son—Mark 1:9–11); and to identify with the sinners He came to save (Jesus' mission was to make unrighteous sinners righteous—Matt. 3:15).

Providing Evidence That Jesus Is the Messiah

As his third task in Israel's spiritual preparation, John provided evidence that Jesus is the Messiah. John's first words in Matthew's Gospel are "Repent, for the kingdom of heaven is near" (3:2). A kingdom is ruled by a king, so John could have drawn on the theme of the kingship of the Messiah (see Psalm 2; 110:1; Isa. 9:6–7; Jer. 23:5–6; Mic. 5:2).

John linked Jesus to the Scriptures by the titles he ascribed to Jesus. Twice John referred publicly to Jesus as "the Lamb of God" (John 1:29, 36). The phrase "Lamb of God" would immediately move a Jewish person's thoughts to the Passover (Exodus 12). Referring to Jesus as Lamb of God meant that Jesus was sinless and therefore qualified to be the only sufficient sacrifice for sin. By saying that Jesus is "the Lamb of God, who takes away the sin of *the world*" (John 1:29), John revealed that the Messiah's work of salvation was not merely national but global.

When John baptized Jesus, he saw the Holy Spirit descend in the form of a dove on Jesus. In affirming the experience, he testified that Jesus "is the Son of God" (v. 34). Earlier John had testified, "He who comes after me has surpassed me because he was before me" (v. 15), implying that Jesus has an eternal existence. Only God is eternal. Therefore, Jesus is more than merely human—He is both God and man.

Eventually Jesus' ministry became more popular than John's (3:22–26). John's followers seemed to resent this, since their leader had been the one to draw attention to Jesus in the first place. But John responded to their comments with wisdom and joy, referring to Jesus as the "bridegroom" and himself as the "best man" (vv. 27–30). John knew the Scriptures and would have been familiar with the concept of God's relationship to Israel as that of a groom and his bride (Psalm 45; Isa. 54:5; 62:4–5; Jer. 2:2; Ezek. 16:8; Hosea 2:19–20). Applying the title of bridegroom to the Messiah may have been original to John, but Jesus certainly applied it to Himself (Matt. 9:15; 25:1–13; Mark 2:19–20; Luke 5:34–35). John intended His hearers to understand that in Jesus, God was seeking afresh to woo and win His bride.

Encouraging Godly Living

Finally, in preparing Israel spiritually for her Messiah, John encouraged people to live godly lives. An individual's repentance and baptism were not to be a momentary experience; they were to permanently influence his or her character and conduct. Luke lets us see some of the responses to John's preaching (3:10–14). The crowd asked, "What should we do then?" John replied that people should be generous with what God gives them, sharing with those in need. God's forgiveness should end selfishness. John indicated that changed lives should transform a community, so that everyone has enough.

Tax collectors listened to John, repented, and were baptized! Probably everyone thought that tax collectors should repent (they were notorious for gouging their fellow Jews and then denying it). John insisted that the tax collectors be models of honesty. An honest tax collector was a contradiction of terms in that day. Righteous living meant an end to hypocrisy. True repentance produces the fruit of righteousness, which is integrity. Roman soldiers were in John's congregation and they too wanted to know what a post-repentant life should look like.

Often because of their official status, weapons, and seeming omnipresence in daily life, soldiers could use several unethical ways to get money from citizens. John told them not to abuse their position or the citizens but to practice the virtue of contentment. Soldiers were to promote peace, not fear. A right relationship to God results in healthy relationships with others.

Righteousness wasn't expected only from average citizens, tax collectors, and soldiers. John also expected Israel's public leaders to conform to God's standards. When John publicly denounced Herod Antipas for divorcing his wife and then stealing and marrying his brother's wife, Herodias (who was Herod's niece), Herod imprisoned him (vv. 19–20). Eventually John's uncompromising stand for God's truth led to his execution (Mark 6:17–29).

Knowing Who He Was

How did John the Baptist see himself? John's mission was to point to Jesus, but people wanted to know about John (John 1:19–27). The representatives of the religious leaders in Jerusalem asked, "Who are you?" John replied, "I am not the Christ." Part of knowing who we are is knowing who we are not. Every Christian, every pastor, every missionary, every church leader needs to learn to say, "I am not the Christ." Only Jesus is the Messiah, the Son of God, and that's why we point to Him. John didn't seek the spotlight and he willingly saw his popularity decline. He was content to be "the voice" preparing for Messiah's coming (v. 23).

When asked if he was Elijah, John said no (v. 21). But Jesus quoted Malachi 3:1 and then said that John *was* "the Elijah who was to come" (Matt. 11:10–14). This sounds contradictory; how can we explain it? John was confident of his identity and he knew he was John, not Elijah. He answered his inquisitors literally: he was really John and he was really not Elijah. Jesus' full statement was "And if you are willing to accept it, he is the Elijah who was to come" (v. 14). Jesus did not mean that John was literally Elijah restored to life, but that his person and work spiritually fulfilled Elijah's prophetic role. Elijah was the type and John was the fulfillment.

Humility marks the character and conduct of John the Baptist. Whenever he spoke of Jesus, he was careful to express that Jesus was the greater one. Jesus had a greater position; John wasn't worthy to carry Jesus' sandals, a task the lowest slave would perform. Jesus exercised a greater power; John baptized with water, but Jesus would baptize with the Holy Spirit and fire (3:11).

John proved his humble spirit when his disciples complained that Jesus was eclipsing John's popularity (John 3:22–26). He compared Jesus to the bridegroom and himself to the best man. As best man, he was full of joy because people were paying attention to Jesus, the One who deserved honor (vv. 27–29). Then John expressed a desire that should be true for every follower of Jesus: "He must become greater; I must become less" (v. 30). The King James Version puts it this way: "He must increase, but I must decrease." John even encouraged his disciples to leave him and follow Jesus. John pointed out Jesus to two of his followers and said, "Look, the Lamb of God!" The two men went off and spent the day with Jesus (1:35–42). One of them was Andrew, and after he brought Peter to Jesus, the two became permanent disciples of the Savior.

John's imprisonment created some doubts in his heart and mind, so he sent some of his disciples to ask Jesus, "Are you the one who was to come, or should we expect someone else?" (Luke 7:19). John was really asking, "Did I get it right in identifying you as the Messiah?" Jesus graciously listened and sent John's disciples back to report what Jesus was doing: the blind see, the lame walk, lepers are cured, the deaf can hear, the dead are raised, and the poor are hearing the good news. (Most of those actions were prophesied by Isaiah in 29:18–19; 35:5–6; 61:1). After John's followers left, Jesus affirmed that John was indeed a prophet, fulfilling Malachi 3:1 and that John was the greatest of the prophets. John didn't know Jesus held him in such high regard. After John was martyred, King Herod heard about Jesus' miracles and thought John had been raised from the dead (Mark 6:16). When others identify us with Jesus, it means we are doing the mission right.

What should we learn from this survey of John the Baptist's life and work?

- Our mission is to point to Jesus.
- We must be content with who we are and what we are called to do.
- We must grow smaller so Jesus can grow greater.
- Speaking God's truth may result in suffering (it's worth it).
- Only Jesus can accurately measure our service to Him.

❧ See: Elijah, Elizabeth, Jesus, Mary, Messiah, Songs, Zechariah

JOSEPH

Two men named Joseph ministered to Jesus, one at the beginning of His earthly ministry—Joseph of Nazareth—and the other at the end of His life on earth—Joseph of Arimathea (John 19:38–42). The first was there for His birth and the second after His death. The first was poor while the second was rich, but both of them were God's chosen servants. For our purposes in this book, we will look at Joseph, the man who was Jesus' foster father on earth.

Joseph the Man

It is generally agreed that the genealogy in Matthew 1 is that of Joseph and the one in Luke 3:23–38 is Mary's. Mary and Joseph both belonged to the house of David.

Joseph is called "a righteous man" (Matt. 1:19), which means he respected the Jewish law and sought to obey it. This is clearly seen in Luke 2:21–40 when he and Mary brought Jesus to the temple for His circumcision and then His dedication. Joseph was also accustomed to celebrating Passover each year in Jerusalem (vv. 41–51).

The people called Jesus "the carpenter's son" (Matt. 13:55), which means that Joseph worked with his hands and was known among the people. He made and repaired things made of wood, such as furniture, carts, and plows. (Houses were generally made of the plentiful stones available in Israel and plastered with mortar.) The fact that Joseph and Mary offered the least expensive sacrifices in the temple suggests that Joseph was a poor man (Luke 2:24; Leviticus 12). For our sakes, Jesus became poor (2 Cor. 8:9).

Joseph the Husband

Mary was probably in her mid-teens when her parents (or guardians) consented to her entering into engagement to marry Joseph. We commend them for looking at Joseph's character and not his income and we commend him for desiring a spiritual wife like Mary. During the year of engagement, they were looked on as husband and wife (see Deut. 22:23–24; Matt. 1:20), and the only way to break the engagement was to get a divorce. This is what Joseph planned to do when he discovered that Mary was pregnant, but God intervened and told him in a dream what he should do (vv. 18–25). Joseph seems to have been a patient man who didn't make decisions impulsively; however, when he knew what God wanted him to do, he obeyed immediately. This entire situation was surely misunderstood by people and gave the town gossips something to talk about. Some students think that the statement addressed to Jesus in John 8:41, "We are not illegitimate children," was meant to slander Him by questioning His birth. Joseph was a man of faith and courage who loved his wife and obeyed his Lord.

Joseph the Foster Father of Jesus

When Mary and Joseph married, Joseph became the legal father of Jesus and therefore had authority to name the child

(Matt. 1:24–25). Note that Joseph's genealogy calls Joseph "the husband of Mary, of whom was born Jesus, who is called Christ" (v. 16). Luke 3:23 says, "He [Jesus] was the son, so it was thought, of Joseph," and that phrase can be translated "as accounted by law" or "as written in the family register." During His ministry, Jesus was called "the son of Joseph" by the people, but they didn't understand that Jesus came into the world through a miraculous birth (4:22; John 1:45; 6:42; see also Matt. 13:55).

By taking Jesus as his own son, Joseph gave Him a legal name, the name God had commanded—Jesus (1:25; Luke 1:31; 2:21). Joseph also provided the care and protection both Mary and the baby needed in those dangerous times. He took them down to Egypt when King Herod was seeking to kill Jesus, and when they returned to Israel, he took them to Nazareth to live. Whenever God gave directions to Joseph, he listened and obeyed. As the Lord Jesus grew up, Joseph taught Him his trade and He was known as "the carpenter" (Mark 6:1–3). That passage also tells us that Mary and Joseph had other children (see Luke 8:19–21; John 7:5). There is no record that Joseph the carpenter ever preached a sermon or did a miracle, but as a faithful Jew, a loving husband, and godly parent, he served the Lord and glorified Him.

> ❦ See: Dreams, Egypt, Genealogy, Mary, Opportunity, Virgin Birth

JOY

Almost every traditional Christmas carol includes such words as *joy, joyful, rejoice, glad, gladness,* and *merry,* because the birth of Jesus Christ was a joyful occasion for the whole world. God had fulfilled His promises and the Savior at last had come. During this season, people greet one another with "Merry Christmas" or "Happy Holidays." In the original Greek text of the

New Testament, the words *joy* and *rejoice* occur 132 times, which tells us that the gospel is a joyful message and living the Christian life should be a joyful experience.

Is there a difference between joy and happiness? Most dictionaries say that there is, for *joy* is defined as "a deep-rooted rapturous emotion . . . so great as to be almost painful in its intensity."[2] *Happiness*, however, depends primarily on happenings. We're happy when everything is going well for us. Joy, however, fills our heart even when circumstances are difficult. People who are outer-directed are happy when circumstances are favorable; people who are inner-directed—meaning having faith in Christ—are joyful even when circumstances are unfavorable. They can say with Paul, "I have learned to be content whatever the circumstances" (Phil. 4:11).

For Christian believers, joy comes from the Holy Spirit within them and not from the happy situation around them, for "the fruit of the Spirit is love, joy, peace" (Gal. 5:22). It is "joy given by the Holy Spirit" (1 Thess. 1:6), the very joy of Christ Himself who prayed that we might have the "full measure" of His joy within us (John 17:13). This joy isn't something that we manufacture or imagine; it's the miraculous fruit of God's life within us. "For the kingdom of God is not a matter of eating and drinking, but of righteousness, peace and joy in the Holy Spirit" (Rom. 14:17).

People may forget their problems and be happy during the Christmas season as they gather together, receive gifts, and enjoy good food, but their happiness usually doesn't last. People glibly say "Merry Christmas" and probably don't realize that the word *merry* comes from a Germanic word that means "short." But to Christian believers, the joy of Christmas isn't a temporary thing, for they may experience Christ's joy every day, all year long. "Rejoice in the Lord always. I will say it again: Rejoice!" (Phil. 4:4). This joy permeates their lives so they have joyful faith and hope and they can rejoice in their trials (Rom. 5:1–5;

2. *Merriam Webster's Dictionary of Synonyms* (1984), 614.

12:12). They pray joyfully (Phil. 1:4) and rejoice even in their sorrows (2 Cor. 6:10). It's a joy that the unbelieving world can't understand or explain.

Let's meet the individuals in the Christmas narrative who experienced the joy of the Lord because of Jesus Christ.

Mary, the Mother of Jesus

Mary was greeted by the angel Gabriel with, "Joy to you who are highly graced" (Luke 1:28, literal translation). Later Simeon would reveal the sorrow that would accompany her honor (2:34–35), but there certainly was joy in her being named the human channel through whom the promised Messiah would come into the world. Her beautiful song of praise (1:46–55) opens with, "My soul glorifies the Lord and my spirit rejoices in God my Savior." Her song reveals not only her joyful saving faith in the Lord but also her knowledge of the Old Testament, for she reflects truths from the song of Hannah (1 Sam. 2:1–10) as well as from several psalms. The Word of God is always a source of joy to the people of God who read and meditate on it (Jer. 15:16). When we submit to God's will as Mary did (Luke 1:38), we experience the joy of the Lord in a special way.

Elizabeth, Zechariah, and John

By God's grace and power, Elizabeth, an elderly, barren wife became a happy mother of a famous son (Ps. 113:9; Luke 1:5–25, 39–45). Hearing Mary's greeting, Elizabeth was filled with the Spirit and expressed her praise, and the son in her womb leaped for joy! Obstetricians today are learning a great deal about external influences on an unborn child. John was also filled with the Spirit (v. 15) and many years later would confess his joy in Jesus Christ (John 3:27–30). John brought much joy to his parents, and the neighbors also rejoiced at the birth of this child (Luke 1:14, 58). When John was eight days old, his father Zechariah regained the ability to hear and speak and sang a joyful song of praise to the Lord (vv. 67–79).

The Angels

The apostle Peter tells us that the angels desire to learn more about God's great plan of salvation (1 Pet. 1:10–12). Two of the angels had temporarily come with Jesus to earth to visit Abraham (Genesis 18), but what did the angels think when they learned that the Son of God would go to earth, be born in a human body, and die in great pain and humiliation? When the angels announced to the shepherds that the Savior had been born, they called it "good news of great joy" (Luke 2:10–12), and indeed it was—and it still is! The angels in heaven rejoice today whenever a sinner repents and turns to Christ for salvation (15:7, 10).

The Shepherds

The word *rejoice* isn't used to describe the shepherds, but surely there was joy in their hearts as they shared the "good news of great joy" with others (Luke 2:17–20). After beholding the newborn Messiah, the shepherds returned to their difficult work with new hope and enthusiasm, for the joy of the Lord was their strength (Neh. 8:10).

The Magi

The journey of the Magi had been a long and difficult one as they followed the star, assuming that the King of the Jews would be born in Jerusalem, the capital city. How disappointed they must have been when they learned that King Herod knew nothing about the birth of a king! The chief priests and teachers of the law knew the prophecy in Micah 5:2 and directed the Magi to Bethlehem (but didn't go themselves!), and the star went before them to lead them to the very house where Mary,

Joseph, and Jesus were living. "When [the Magi] saw the star, they were overjoyed" (Matt. 2:10).

We are not likely to hear angels or see a dazzling star, but the joy of Christ's birth can still thrill our hearts as we worship the Son of God who is King of Kings and Lord of Lords.

🕯 **See: Elizabeth, Greetings, Mary, Shepherds, Songs**

KING

The word *king* transports Americans into an unfamiliar world. U.S. citizens vote for or against candidates for office. If the official performs poorly, he or she can be voted out of office. Monarchy is a different political reality from democracy. Kings are not elected. By hereditary right a king assumes the throne and is monarch for life. The king is sovereign; he has the authority and power to carry out his decisions, and his will must be obeyed. When monarchs ruled the nations, they were said to do so by the "divine right of kings," meaning God placed the monarch on his throne.

In the Old Testament, kings were referred to as "shepherds" (see Ezekiel 34; Mic. 5:1, 4) and had the responsibility to care for, protect, and lead the people of the nation. The king as shepherd was to be a responsible leader who served the people under God's authority. The people were not to be abused for the king's benefit; the king was to bless the people.

Israel's experience of monarchy was inconsistent. David was a king after God's own heart, but Solomon turned from God to enhance his own power and comfort. Over the years, more

121

kings followed idols than followed Jehovah, to the nation's decline. Even when Israel's king was good, he died eventually. At the time of Jesus' birth, the tyrannical Herod the Great reigned over Israel. "Kings is mostly rapscallions" is what Mark Twain said through Huck Finn, and history supports the conclusion. Of course, he was speaking of human kings.

At Jesus' birth, only the Magi spoke of Him as a king (Matt. 2:2), although Mary knew that God would give her Son the throne of His father David (Luke 1:32). When he was called to discipleship, Nathanael referred to Jesus as "the King of Israel" (John 1:49). "Son of David" was how some persons addressed Jesus (Matt. 12:23; 15:22; Luke 18:39), and at His triumphal entry, the people shouted "Hosanna to the Son of David" (Matt. 21:9, 15). As the Son of David, Jesus was and is rightful heir to the throne God promised to King David (2 Sam. 7:11b, 16).

Israel's prophets wrote about a coming king, in the line of David, one who had all the right qualities and character of royalty:

> For to us a child is born, to us a son is given, and the government will be on his shoulders. And he will be called Wonderful Counselor, Mighty God, Everlasting Father, Prince of Peace. Of the increase of his government and peace there will be no end. He will reign on David's throne and over his kingdom, establishing and upholding it with justice and righteousness from that time on and forever. The zeal of the LORD Almighty will accomplish this.
>
> *Isaiah 9:6–7*

> But you, Bethlehem Ephrathah, though you are small among the clans of Judah, out of you will come for me one who will be ruler over Israel, whose origins are from of old, from ancient times. . . . He will stand and shepherd his flock in the strength of the LORD, in the majesty of the name of the LORD his God. And they will live securely, for then his greatness will reach to the ends of the earth. And he will be their peace.
>
> *Micah 5:2, 4–5*

According to Isaiah and Micah, the coming King belongs to David's line and this King will rule according to God's character and law. Peace will be the hallmark of this King's reign, and the people He rules will enjoy justice, righteousness, and security. "The government will be on his shoulders" implies that this King alone is responsible for governing and that He alone has authority to reign. Here is a King to be trusted and honored! This is King Jesus.

What kind of king is King Jesus?

King Jesus defeats His enemies and He defeats them so they stay defeated. Jesus has conquered sin, death, Satan, and hell. King Jesus establishes peace, not only ending war but providing adequate resources for His people. Jesus is a King who loves His people. He graciously meets their needs, heals their wounds, and hears and answers their requests. The subjects of King Jesus always have access to Him. King Jesus secures justice for His people. Legally justice means resolving differences fairly; law and grace are always perfectly balanced in King Jesus' court. Justice in the Old Testament includes a relational dimension. Under King Jesus, His subjects don't merely coexist, they thrive together. King Jesus is wise. He doesn't always reveal what He is doing and He works at many levels of life simultaneously to achieve His purposes over time. He knows the end from the beginning, so His plans always work to perfection.

The reign of King Jesus is eternal. Because His position is permanent, His subjects don't have to worry about changes in policy or law. King Jesus lives forever, so there is no worry about His growing old or dying. Under King Jesus, there will be glorious, multifaceted continuity. Jesus is the only King who is worthy of worship forever. He suffered for our sake on the cross and rose again to give life eternal. King Jesus is His people's treasure, their source of endless joy and eternal delight.

How should we act in the presence of a king? Reverently—with open ears and closed mouth. Submissively—the proper posture in the presence of the King is to kneel. And boldly—Jesus is the King who loves us, who knows us completely. He wants us to enjoy a respectful intimacy with Him. (What is it like at your church when you enter the sanctuary for worship? Is there a sense of the King's presence?)

King Jesus is without equal and He tolerates no rival. Only Jesus truly has the "divine right" of kings because only He is fully God and fully human, the rightful heir of David's throne. He is "KING OF KINGS AND LORD OF LORDS" (Rev. 19:16). All hail King Jesus!

𝑒 See: David, Genealogy, Immanuel, Messiah, Prophecy

LIFE

Christmas is the celebration of the birth of Jesus Christ, and birth makes us think of life. Jesus was born from His mother's womb as any child, but He also "came into the world" as no other child because He had existed before the universe was created. Seven times in the Gospel of John, Jesus is quoted as saying that He "came down from heaven" (3:13; 6:33, 38, 42, 50–51, 58). Babies receive life from their parents, but Jesus had life in Himself. "In the beginning was the Word, and the Word was with God, and the Word was God. . . . In him was life, and that life was the light of men" (1:1, 4). Jesus boldly said, "For as the Father has life in himself, so he has granted the Son to have life in himself" (5:26). Because Jesus has life in Himself, He is able to give eternal life to all who trust Him.

The apostle John wrote, "The life appeared; we have seen it and testify to it, and we proclaim to you the eternal life which was with the Father and has appeared to us" (1 John 1:2). When people looked at Jesus, they were seeing the Father who sent Him (John 14:1–14). "Christ Jesus came into the world to save sinners," wrote Paul (1 Tim. 1:15), and John wrote, "And we have seen and testify that the Father has sent his Son to be the Savior of the world" (1 John 4:14). Savior from what? From sin, because "the wages of sin is death, but the gift of God is eternal life in Jesus Christ our Lord" (Rom. 6:23). Jesus said, "I have come that they may have life, and have it to the full" (John 10:10).

Scientists have a difficult time defining life but they know what it takes to sustain life: light, air, water, and food. Jesus is the light of life (8:12) and He provides the breath of life (20:21–22), the water of life (4:10; 7:38), and the bread of life (6:51, 58). Peter wrote, "His divine power has given us everything we need for life and godliness" (2 Pet. 1:3). Everything! To receive Jesus into your life means you have all that you need for time and eternity. We have a living hope (1 Pet. 1:3), the living word (v. 23), and access to God through "a new and living way" (Heb. 10:20). We need not fear life or death because Jesus is "the resurrection and the life" (John 11:25–26).

ὲ See: Faith, Immanuel, Overshadow, Virgin Birth

LIGHT

The celebration of Christmas is associated with lights. People decorate their homes with strings of colored lights, both inside and outside, and the smallest towns join the largest cities in stringing lights in the shopping districts to help encourage "the Christmas spirit." Even the president of the United States leaves the Oval Office and hosts the public lighting of the official White House Christmas tree.

Christmas lights are more than decorations; they are also reminders of what happened that first Christmas. When Jesus Christ was born, the world was shrouded in darkness and imprisoned by the fear of death. "The people living in darkness have seen a great light; on those living in the land of the shadow of death a light has dawned," says Matthew 4:16, quoting Isaiah 9:2. "I have come into the world as a light," said Jesus, "so that no one who believes in me should stay in darkness" (John 12:46). That's the third and last time in the Gospel of John that Jesus referred to Himself as "the light of the world" (see John 8:12; 9:5).

The only literal "light of the world" we have is the sun, the center of our universe and a symbol of our God (Ps. 84:11; Mal. 4:2). God's glory is compared to that of the sun (Matt. 17:2; Acts 26:13–15; Rev. 1:16), and the light of the sun is what brings life to the earth. If the sun ceased shining, life on earth would die; and if its light and heat were intensified, everything living would burn up. Zechariah the priest compared the birth of Jesus to the dawning of a new day for a world in darkness. The Lord would "give his people the knowledge of salvation through the forgiveness of their sins, because of the tender mercy of our God, by which the rising sun will come to us from heaven to shine on those living in darkness and in the shadow of death, to guide our feet into the path of peace" (Luke 1:77–79). You can tell he was acquainted with Isaiah 9.

The light of God's glory awakened and alarmed the shepherds, and the angel's glad tidings motivated them to go to Bethlehem to see the Savior. The light of the star guided the wise men to Jerusalem, and the light of Micah's prophecy, along with the star, directed them to the Savior in Bethlehem (Matt. 2:1–12; 2 Pet. 1:19). The shepherds and the wise men could say to the Lord along with David "in your light we see light" (Ps. 36:9). Because God sent the light of His glory, the light of the star, and the light of His Word, the shepherds and wise men were able to see the Light of the world.

The aged Simeon looked at Jesus and said to the Lord, "For my eyes have seen your salvation, which you have prepared in the sight of all people, a light for revelation to the Gentiles and for glory to your people Israel" (Luke 2:30–32). The light of God's glory had not been on the earth since it departed from the temple in the days of the Jewish captivity (Ezek. 10–11) but now it had returned! "The Word became flesh and made his dwelling among us. We have seen his glory, the glory of the One and Only, who came from the Father, full of grace and truth" (John 1:14). But the light of salvation was also for the Gentiles, for Matthew applied Isaiah's prophecy to the Gentiles (Matt. 4:12–17). Jesus is indeed "the light of the world" and "the Savior of the world" (1 John 4:14).

Why don't needy, lost sinners see this Light and by faith receive the gift of salvation? Some have never heard the "glad tidings of great joy," and it's our responsibility to tell them. Some are making excuses instead of being honest with themselves and with the Lord. And some have walked in moral and spiritual darkness for so long that they refuse to face the light. "This is the verdict: Light has come into the world, but men loved darkness instead of light because their deeds were evil. Everyone who does evil hates the light, and will not come into the light for fear that his deeds will be exposed" (John 3:19–20).

This Christmas will you be able to "declare the praises of him who called you out of darkness into his wonderful light" (1 Pet. 2:9)? Or haven't you yet responded to His call?

❧ Advent, Angels, Glory, Life, Shepherds, Simeon, Wise Men, World

LOVE

The New Testament Greek language had at least four words for *love*. English has one. *Love* is a word that must be regularly reinvested with meaning to keep it rich and weighty. The Bible accomplishes this task. The highest word for love in the New Testament, *agape* (ἀγάπη), means to choose to do what is best for the other person. This kind of love is primarily an act of the will; it is love that chooses to sacrifice itself for others. This defines God's love for us: "an unconditional commitment to an imperfect person."[3] God does not merely have affection for us; He wills to achieve our good for His glory.

3. H. Norman Wright, *Premarital Counseling* (Chicago: Moody Press, 1977), 86.

Ponder these twenty-first-century beliefs (misbeliefs) about "love":

- If you love me, you'll give me what I want.
- If you love me, you won't allow me to hurt.
- If you love me, you'll let me bend the rules.
- If you love me, you won't make me change.

Contrast these misbeliefs about love with the truth about God's love:

- Because God loves us, He gives us what we need but He will not spoil us.
- Because God loves us, He does let us experience pain. It may be the pain of disciplining us for disobeying. It may be suffering that produces maturity. Or it may be the relational hurt that comes from the fact that every person is a sinner.
- Because God loves us, He enforces His rules. He teaches us what is right, He corrects us when we are wrong, and He develops self-disciplined children who choose righteousness.
- Because God loves us, He is committed to a lifelong process of transforming us into the image of His Son (Rom. 8:29). That means removing our sinfulness and instilling Christ's holiness. Change is unavoidable.

How do we know God loves us? To begin with, the incarnation and the birth of Christ make His love evident (Titus 3:4–5; 1 John 4:9–10). Second, the death of Christ on the cross shows His amazing love (John 3:16). Third, God sent His Son while we were His enemies (Rom. 5:8), so it had to be His love that compelled Him. Next, we know God's love through the experience of new life in Christ (Eph. 2:4–5). Finally, He promises that nothing can separate us from the love of God in Christ (Rom. 8:38–39).

Those actions are affirmed by God's words to us. Throughout the entire Bible, God is telling us, "I love you." Love needs to be spoken clearly and love needs to be shown convincingly. God does both perfectly.

How can we love God back? What reveals our love? First John 4:14–21 provides the answers:

> And we have seen and testify that the Father has sent his Son to be the Savior of the world. If anyone acknowledges that Jesus is the Son of God, God lives in him and he in God. And so we know and rely on the love God has for us.
>
> God is love. Whoever lives in love lives in God, and God in him. In this way, love is made complete among us so that we will have confidence on the day of judgment, because in this world we are like him. There is no fear in love. But perfect love drives out fear, because fear has to do with punishment. The one who fears is not made perfect in love.
>
> We love because he first loved us. If anyone says, "I love God," yet hates his brother, he is a liar. For anyone who does not love his brother, whom he has seen, cannot love God, whom he has not seen. And he has given us this command: Whoever loves God must also love his brother.

One way we show God that we love Him is by our confession of Jesus as the Savior of the world and as the Son of God (vv. 14–15). Another way we express our love to God is by our connection to Christ. The word *lives* in verse 15 is translated "abides" in other versions. The word *abide* reminds us of Jesus' teaching about the vital link between the vine and branches in John 15. The connection between Jesus and His followers is necessary for life and to produce spiritual fruit.

The confidence we have in Christ (v. 17) is another way we demonstrate our love for God. John says that fear is evidence that we doubt God's love. In a healthy marriage, a husband and wife rest securely in each other's love. They don't take love for granted but they do not doubt it either. A healthy, growing relationship to Christ is revealed by an unshakeable confidence in God's love.

Finally, our love for God is demonstrated by our conduct toward God's people. Our relationships to our fellow believers reveal whether we love God. It is easier to say "I love you" than it is to show it, and the apostle John warned against the hypocrisy of words without loving actions (3:18).

Is *love* a magnificent word to you? Are you convinced that God loves you? Does God know that you love Him?

❦ See: Advent, Gifts, Grace, Holy Spirit

MANGER

In ancient Palestine, many houses had a lower level that was divided, one side being the family sleeping area, the other being the pen for the animals. The animals may have added a certain aromatic element but they also provided warmth. A manger—a feeding trough—would have been a normal and necessary piece of equipment where animals were kept.

Was the manger where Jesus lay made of stone? Or was it made of wood? We don't know. Was the manger filled with hay or straw? Surely Joseph cleaned out any remains of what the animals had been feeding on and replaced it with something soft and fresh. But we don't know. A manger would have been big enough to hold an infant, and that was Jesus' first cradle (Luke 2:7).

It must have been unusual to put a newborn baby in a manger, because that was one of the signs the angel gave to the shepherds for finding the Christ Child (v. 12). Evidently the shepherds knew the places in Bethlehem that would have a manger, and they found Joseph, Mary, and Jesus without difficulty (v. 16).

The manger tells us of the poverty of Jesus. Joseph and Mary couldn't buy their way into nicer quarters (if they had been available). They had just the necessities as they began family life, but what they had was enough.

The manger also reminds us of the humility of Jesus. He was the King of Glory who left heaven's throne to be enthroned in a feeding trough. Surely the Son of God deserved better than this! But He did not demand it. He is God stooping to identify with sinful humanity, coming as one of the lowest of the low. The big theological word for this is "condescension." It is best expressed in Philippians 2:6–7: "Who, being in very nature God, did not consider equality with God something to be grasped, but made himself nothing, taking the very nature of a servant, being found in appearance as a man."

❦ See: Bethlehem, Immanuel, Inn, Shepherds

MARY

There is an appropriate mystery to the virginal conception. We are told that the Holy Spirit "overshadowed" Mary, causing her womb to conceive and the Son of God to take on flesh. The Spirit's overshadowing was the process that enabled Mary to conceive while ensuring that the Child would be holy (Luke 1:35).

While we cannot precisely know all the reasons God chose Mary to be the mother of the Christ Child, the Gospel narratives give us important insights.

Gabriel was sent to a *virgin* (vv. 26–27), implying that Mary was sexually pure, and we assume that she pursued purity of mind and soul as well as body. When she understood Gabriel's message, she asked how the conception would happen, because she was a virgin. Mary clearly affirmed her sexual purity.

A Person God Could Choose

Mary did not claim to be sinless, however. In her great song of worship, the Magnificat (vv. 46–55), she refers to God as "my Savior" (v. 47), thereby acknowledging that she was a sinner in need of God's salvation. While she gave a human body and nature to the Lord Jesus, her sin nature was not passed on by virtue of the Spirit's overshadowing. *God chooses and uses persons who are pure.*

Mary demonstrated a great reverence for God. When Gabriel appeared, she did not seem stunned by the reality of angelic beings. Rather, she seems to have been trying to figure out why God would send an angel to her. In the Magnificat she called God "the Lord," "God my Savior," and "the Mighty One," then celebrated God's holiness, mercy, power, and promise keeping. In verse 50 she quotes Psalm 103:17, referring to those who "fear him." Mary was one of those in Israel who truly feared God. She honored, respected, and worshiped Him and Him alone. Because of her reverence for God, she embraced the will of God, calling herself "the Lord's servant" (Luke 1:38). Her reverence for God made her a joyful woman. *God chooses and uses persons who fear Him.*

Her firm grasp of Scripture, and its grip on her, set Mary apart from most others. Her character, her worldview, her understanding of history and future events were all shaped by God's Word. Again, the Magnificat reveals what was in Mary's heart and mind. Her song is shaped by Hannah's words of praise to God in 1 Samuel 2. It draws from a number of psalms and the book of Job and ends by referring to God's promises to Abraham in Genesis 17. Mary had paid attention to the Scriptures, she had internalized them, and she had obeyed them. When God chose her to bring the Messiah into the world, her response is expressed in biblical phrases, images, and references. She believed God's Word was true, and she saw her own experience as fulfillment of divine promises. *God chooses and uses persons who love and live His Word.*

Because Mary reverenced God and because she honored His Word, she had a submissive spirit. She listened to Gabriel's message, raised her honest question, listened carefully to Gabriel's response, and then said, "I am the Lord's servant" (Luke 1:38). Surely Mary had more questions to ask, especially about how her pregnancy would affect her relationships to Joseph, her family,

and the Nazareth community. Others might have chosen to argue
or demand assurances. Not Mary. Her life was lived for God,
under God's Word, and she unhesitatingly agreed to serve God's
purpose. *God chooses and uses persons with a submissive spirit.*

A Person of Faith

Mary's faith in God is expressed in how she allowed God to
convince Joseph of the truth of her condition. In Matthew's
Gospel (1:18–25) we learn that Joseph and Mary were engaged
prior to her becoming pregnant and that Joseph knew he wasn't
the father. It is also clear that Joseph loved Mary and agonized
over divorcing her (engagement among the Jews at that time
imposed the exclusiveness of marriage on the couple with none
of the privileges). Through an angel's message in a dream, God
directed Joseph to the right decision.

It seems equally clear that Mary loved Joseph (they eventually had a rather large family; see Mark 6:3). Mary's faith in
God kept her faithful to Joseph when he wasn't sure what to
do. Together Mary and Joseph had to face their families and
the wagging tongues in Nazareth when her pregnancy became
obvious. They knew the truth—but who would believe them?
So Joseph and Mary absorbed the gossip and looks and unkind
treatment that came their way. For God's sake, and the truth's
sake, they were faithful under pressure.

Mary and Joseph had faith that Caesar's decree, which required them to travel to Bethlehem, was God's plan. They trusted
God when Mary's labor started, when Jesus was born, when
shepherds came, when Magi arrived, and when they had to leave
for Egypt. They trusted God when He told them to return to the
land of Israel. Over time, they built a good marriage and raised
their family. *God chooses and uses persons who are faithful.*

Maturity is a word that accurately describes Mary, although
she was likely not much older than sixteen. Her awareness of
God, her confidence in Scripture, her understanding of relationships, and her courage despite opposition reveal a woman with

deep roots ready to face realistically life's joys and sorrows. She had an amazing capacity to adjust to God's directives and life's changing circumstances.

A Loving Mother and Disciple

Mary was a good mother. From the account of Jesus in the temple at age twelve (Luke 2:41–51), we know that Joseph and Mary raised Jesus to keep the Law and know the Scriptures. They taught Him to think and to ask good questions and to obey His parents. Jesus learned Joseph's craft and evidently supported the family after Joseph died (since Jesus was known as "the carpenter"—Mark 6:3; if Joseph were still alive, he would have been "the carpenter").

Mary endured the pain of seeing her Son suffer and die on the cross. Simeon predicted that a sword would pierce Mary's soul because of Jesus (Luke 2:35). It did, and Mary did not flinch.

Mary is a model disciple. She must have asked herself, *Who is this?* as she watched and listened to Jesus as He grew up. Her internal quest to understand what it meant for the Word to become flesh must have been intense. As Jesus' mother, she knew who He was: God's Son in human form.

Mary's last recorded words in Scripture are, "Do whatever he tells you" (John 2:5). Our final glimpse of Mary in Scripture is in Acts 1, where she is one of the believers gathered for prayer in the upper room (1:14). She was saved by faith in the child she had carried in her womb, whom she had raised, whom she saw die, and who she knew was risen from the dead.

🕮 See: Faith, Immanuel, Jesus, Joseph, Joy, Overshadow, Questions, Simeon, Songs, Tears, Virgin Birth

MESSIAH

The Hebrew word *mashiah* means "anointed one." The Greek equivalent is *christos* and gives us the word "Christ," which is used more than five hundred times in the New Testament. Whenever we say "Jesus Christ," we are saying "Jesus the Messiah, Jesus the Anointed One."

The Messiah is the Redeemer for whom the Jewish nation had been waiting and through whom they expected to be freed from their enemies and brought into the promised kingdom. Even today, in many Hebrew prayer books, the Thirteen Articles of Faith conclude with: "I believe with a perfect heart that the Messiah will come; and although his coming be delayed, I will still wait patiently for his speedy appearance" (see Ps. 2:1–2; Dan. 9:25–26; Matt. 22:41–46; Acts 4:23–30).

The title *Messiah* reveals several important truths about Jesus.

His Person: Jesus Is God

To call Jesus "the Christ" or "the Son of David" is to call Him "Son of God." Matthew's Gospel opens with, "A record of the genealogy of Jesus Christ the son of David" (1:1); and Mark calls Him "Jesus Christ, the Son of God" (1:1). At the close of Luke's Gospel, Jesus calls Himself "the Christ" and states that the Old Testament Scriptures teach about Him (24:26, 46). John wrote his Gospel so that people might believe "that Jesus is the Christ, the Son of God" and have "life in his name" (John 20:31). The people in Jerusalem lauded Him as "the Son of David" (Matt. 20:30; 21:9, 15). Andrew and John confessed that Jesus was the Christ (John 1:40–41), as did Peter (Matt. 16:13–16) and Martha (John 11:27).

During our Lord's earthly ministry, the main question was, "Is this Jesus of Nazareth the Messiah, the Christ?" and it was asked by leaders and common people alike. The religious leaders asked Him, "How long will you keep us in suspense? If you are the Christ, tell us plainly" (10:24). The rabbis applied 456 Old Testament passages to the Messiah, and Jesus Himself said, "If you believed Moses, you would believe me, for he wrote about me" (5:46). In his sermon at Pentecost, Peter told the crowd that Jesus was "both Lord and Christ" (Acts 2:36; and see 5:42; 10:36). This was also Paul's message (9:22).

His Offices

Under the Jewish economy, to be anointed was to be set apart for God's exclusive use. The anointing was reserved for the sanctuary of God (Exod. 30:26–30; 40:9–11), the priests who served there (29:21; Lev. 8:30), the prophets of God (1 Kings 19:16), and the kings (1 Sam. 9:16; 16:3; 24:7–11). The special oil used was a symbol of the Holy Spirit of God.

The human body of Jesus was a temple (John 2:18–22), for "in Christ all the fullness of the Deity lives in bodily form" (Col. 2:9). The Father gave the Spirit to Him "without limit" (John 3:34). While ministering here on earth, Jesus was a prophet who spoke forth the Word of God (see Deut. 18:18). Today Jesus ministers in the heavenly sanctuary as the King-Priest "in the order of Melchizedek" (Heb. 7:17; Ps. 110:4; see Hebrews 7–8), and when He returns, He will establish His kingdom and reign as "KING OF KINGS AND LORD OF LORDS" (Rev. 19:16). He is the anointed Prophet, Priest, and King.

His Power

For His sermon in the synagogue in His hometown of Nazareth, Jesus read this text: "The Spirit of the Lord is on me, because he has anointed me to preach good news to the poor. He has sent me to proclaim freedom for the prisoners and recovery of sight for the blind, to release the oppressed, to proclaim the year of the Lord's favor" (Luke 4:18–19, quoted from Isa. 61:1–2). When our Lord lived on earth, all that He did was directed by the Father and empowered by the Holy Spirit, whom the Father gave to Jesus "without limit" (John 3:34; Acts 4:27). "God anointed Jesus of Nazareth with the Holy Spirit and power," said Peter, "and he went around doing good and healing" (10:38).

While ministering on earth, Jesus lived and served just as we His followers must live and serve today: directed by the Word of God, energized by the Holy Spirit, and depending wholly on prayer. He did not use His divine attributes independent of the Father. If we hope to succeed in life and service, no matter what God has called us to do, we must follow that example: prayer, the Word, and the Holy Spirit's power (6:4 and 1:8).

Each member of God's family has the gift of the Holy Spirit and gifts from the Spirit to be used for service (1 Cor. 12:1–11; Eph. 4:1–16). The Spirit has anointed us (2 Cor. 1:21) and the Spirit teaches us the truth so that we can understand the Word and detect the lies of the enemy (1 John 2:20, 27; 4:1–6). We may ask God for wisdom, and He will give it to us (James 1:5). Our privilege is to "keep in step with the Spirit" (Gal. 5:25) and depend on His power as He fills us and enables us to glorify Christ. By God's grace, we possess the anointing. Don't leave home without Him in control.

ò See: Immanuel, Jesus, Nazarene

NAZARENE

When Joseph and Mary brought the child Jesus back to Israel from Egypt, God warned Joseph in a dream not to settle in Judea but to return to their native town of Nazareth in Galilee, about seventy miles from Jerusalem (Matt. 2:19–23; see Luke 1:26–27; 2:4–5). Excavations reveal that Nazareth was not a large city but a humble town of fewer than five hundred people. There are twenty-five references to Nazareth in the New Testament and the word *Nazarene* is found six times. Jesus was known as Jesus of Nazareth or Jesus the Nazarene. Matthew saw in the move to Nazareth a fulfillment of the words of the prophets but he didn't tell us which prophets. We will try to solve the puzzle and also learn some helpful lessons.

The Historical Jesus

Jesus was a real person who grew up in a real place, Nazareth in Galilee. His birth and name were registered (Luke 2:21), and people knew His parents (Joseph was His foster father) and His brothers and sisters (Matt. 1:16; 13:53–58; John 6:42). If you had told anybody in Nazareth that there was no such person as Jesus, they would have laughed at you. They watched Him grow up and saw Him working in Joseph's carpenter shop. Some of them would remember when He suddenly left Nazareth for Judea. Later they heard that He had been baptized in the Jordan River by John the Baptist and had become an itinerant teacher. He returned to Nazareth and preached in the synagogue He had attended most of His life, and the citizens drove Him out of town (Luke 4:14–30). He was a prophet without honor in His own hometown.

The Christian faith is based on solid historical events, including the life of Jesus of Nazareth and His death, burial, resurrection, and ascension. These events form the foundation of the gospel, the good news of salvation through faith in Jesus Christ (1 Cor. 15:1–11; Gal. 1:1–10). To deny this is to deny history.

The Rejected Jesus

"So was fulfilled what was said through the prophets, 'He will be called a Nazarene'" (Matt. 2:23). Students and teachers have wrestled with that statement because this prophecy cannot be found in *one* of the prophetic books, let alone several of them (as the plural "prophets" would imply). To claim that this prophecy has been lost is to say that the Holy Spirit failed to get parts of the inspired Word into Scripture and this is unthinkable (see 5:18). Or to argue that this prophecy was *spoken* but not *written* is refuted by Matthew 2:15, 17, where the verb "spoken" is used, yet the prophecies referred to in these verses were written in Hosea 11:1 and Jeremiah 31:15.

To relate *Nazarene* to the word *Nazirite* is erroneous, because Jesus was not a Nazirite like John the Baptist (Matt. 11:16–19; see Numbers 6; Judg. 13:1–5 for the requirements of Nazirites). Luke records at least two occasions when Jesus touched dead bodies, and this was forbidden to Nazirites (Luke 7:11–17; 8:40–56), and He also drank wine.

Some students believe that the name Nazareth came from the Hebrew *netzer*, which means "a branch or a shoot," and there are prophecies about Jesus that use the image of the branch (Isa. 4:2; 11:1; Jer. 23:5; 33:15; Zech. 3:8; 6:12–13). Some authorities consider this explanation farfetched; and it is probably true that most of the people in Jesus' day connected Nazareth with Nazarene when they referred to Him.

We must not ignore the fact that Matthew wrote "prophets" and not "prophet." New Testament scholar Leon Morris writes: "It appears that Matthew is drawing attention to the thrust of Old Testament prophecy about the Christ rather than to any one passage."[4] What one thing about the Christ did all the Old Testament prophets write about? *He would be despised and rejected by the people.* See Psalm 22:6–8, 13; 69:8, 11, 19–21; 118:22; Isaiah 49:7; 52:13–53:12; Zechariah 13:7–9. His suffering and rejection are also seen in the Old Testament types, such as the Passover lamb (John 1:29; 1 Cor. 5:7) and the uplifted serpent (John 3:14; see Numbers 21).

Many of the people of Judah considered Nazareth a town of backward people whom they despised. When Philip told Nathanael that "Jesus of Nazareth" was the promised Messiah, Nathanael replied, "Nazareth! Can anything good come from there?" (John 1:45–46). In calling Jesus "the Nazarene," people could be identifying His hometown but also ridiculing Him and rejecting His claims. When speaking to Peter, the servant girl called Him "that Nazarene, Jesus" (Mark 14:67). Had He been known as "Jesus of Bethlehem," it would have identified Him with a famous city in Judah where David was born, but He humbled Himself and accepted the title "the Nazarene."

Hebrews 13:11–13 pictures Jesus as the sin offering that was taken outside the camp (Lev. 4:12; 16:21). Just as He was crucified outside the city of Jerusalem, we should "go to him outside the camp, bearing the disgrace he bore" (Heb. 13:13).

---

4. Leon Morris, *The Gospel according to Matthew* (Grand Rapids: Eerdmans, 1992), 49.

- N -

The Obedient Jesus

Twice in the Christmas narrative, Matthew tells us that Joseph was obedient to the Word of the prophets: taking Jesus to Egypt (Matt. 2:13–15) and settling in Nazareth (vv. 21–23). Even wicked King Herod fulfilled prophecy when he had the children slain in Bethlehem (vv. 16–18), and so did the devious priests when they purchased the potter's field (27:1–10). Jesus lived in Nazareth because the Father put Him there.

But six times in his Gospel, Matthew points out that Jesus did certain things that fulfilled what had been prophesied centuries before (4:13–16; 8:17; 12:15–21; 13:34–35; 21:1–5; 26:47–56). Look up these references and see in Jesus an example of how we should live by the Word of God and seek to please the Father.

The Exalted Jesus

As we have seen, our Lord humbled Himself when He allowed people to add Nazarene and Nazareth to His name. But God's promise is that humility leads to exaltation (1 Pet. 5:5–6), and Jesus took the name Nazareth with Him to the cross! Pilate had a sign written in Hebrew, Latin, and Greek that said, "JESUS OF NAZARETH, THE KING OF THE JEWS" (John 19:19). Perhaps the people of Nazareth didn't appreciate this embarrassing public announcement, but those who put their faith in Jesus would eventually glory in the cross (Gal. 6:14).

But Jesus lifted the name of His hometown even higher. Jesus revealed Himself to Saul of Tarsus who was persecuting the church, and Saul asked, "Who are you, Lord?" Jesus answered, "I am Jesus of Nazareth, whom you are persecuting" (Acts 22:8). Jesus spoke the word *Nazareth* from the glories of heaven! The name of Jesus had been exalted to highest heaven—it is "the name that is above every name" (Phil. 2:9)—but in His grace, He still linked it with Nazareth. What a lesson Saul of Tarsus learned that day!

Can anything good come out of Nazareth—or out of our lives? That same Saul, now Paul the apostle, wrote, "I know that nothing good lives in me, that is, in my sinful nature" (Rom. 7:18). But Someone good and gracious *came to Nazareth* and offered the people salvation, and they rejected Him. Jesus has never withdrawn His invitation, yet people continue to reject Him.

Jesus of Nazareth is still passing by (Luke 18:35–43), and He stops to help all who call on Him and trust Him. "And everyone who calls on the name of the Lord will be saved" (Acts 2:21).

❦ See: Immanuel, Jesus, King, Messiah

OPPORTUNITY

An opportunity is "a favorable juncture of circumstances," according to Webster. Opportunities are time sensitive: there is a brief "open window" for deciding and acting. To seize the opportunity may change you, your life, and the world. To refuse the opportunity may mean living with "might-have-beens."

Do you see an opportunity as a fresh adventure or as a disruption to a comfortable life? Saying yes to an opportunity is sure to result in change. Declining an opportunity may only deepen the ruts of routine.

Some of the main characters of the Advent and Christmas stories were presented with amazing opportunities to work with God. Let's briefly explore their experiences, considering the risks and the rewards of a God-given opportunity.

Zechariah and Elizabeth had prayed for a child (Luke 1:13). But when the angel Gabriel told Zechariah that his prayers were answered, he saw the obstacle, their old age (v. 18), instead of the opportunity to trust God. Zechariah became a father but he endured at least nine months of silence for his disbelief.

When he named his son John, Zechariah was given a second opportunity to give praise to God.

Mary's opportunity was to cooperate with God in His Son's entrance into the human race. She could have said no, citing the problems that would come with being single and pregnant. But she chose to submit to God's plan and now she is called "blessed." Seizing her opportunity had a price; the sword did pierce her heart when Jesus was crucified (2:35).

When *Joseph* learned of Mary's pregnancy, he faced a weighty choice, and in that choice was his opportunity. He could privately break off his engagement to Mary or he could go ahead with the marriage but face scandal. After God revealed His plan through a dream, Joseph became Mary's husband and eventually Jesus' earthly stepfather (Matt. 1:18–25). Joseph trained Jesus in Scripture, in the carpenter's craft, and in relationships. Much of what he did for Jesus is unknown to us, but Joseph made the most of his moment.

The *shepherds* outside Bethlehem saw the angel, heard the announcement, and heard the angelic chorus give glory to God. They took the message seriously and went to town searching for the infant Savior in a manger (Luke 2:8–20). Theirs was an opportunity to see God's gift of salvation firsthand and to prove that what God says can be trusted.

Once they saw the miraculous star, the *Magi* knew they had an opportunity to see and worship the King of the Jews. The journey promised to be expensive and hazardous, but they dropped everything and took to the road. Between the guiding star and information about Bethlehem from Jerusalem's biblical experts, the Magi found the Christ Child, presented their gifts, and worshiped the King. They had an opportunity to let Herod know where the child was, but they took God's warning and went home by an alternate route (Matt. 2:1–12). Not every opportunity is worth seizing.

Herod and Israel's religious leaders had an opportunity to welcome the Messiah and be among the first to acknowledge Him as King. But they were protective of their positions and saw the newborn King as a threat. Even though Magi from the

East came seeking this child, and even though the Scriptures identified Bethlehem as the place where Messiah would be born, they refused to see the truth. They knew the Scripture but missed its fulfillment. Eventually Herod had all the boys two years old and younger put to death (vv. 16–18). He missed the spiritual opportunity and embraced the evil one.

What about *us*? Do Advent and Christmas still hold opportunities for us? They do.

- As long as there is life, the opportunity to receive God's gift of salvation through faith in Jesus is available.
- Perhaps you need to take advantage of the opportunity to forgive someone who hurt you and heal the relationship.
- Look for openings to tell the story of God's love during the season.
- Maybe it's time to make a new beginning: turning a character weakness into a strength, obeying where you have been rebellious, or tearing down a stronghold.
- Certainly this season is full of opportunities to pray, to hear or make glorious music, to be silent and meditate on what God is doing in your life, and to give in ways that make a spiritual difference.
- Advent is an opportunity to rekindle hope. After all, we are waiting for a Savior from glory.
- Every day is an opportunity to prepare ourselves to meet the Lord face-to-face.

꙳ See: Herod the Great, Joseph, Mary, Shepherds, Star, Wise Men, Zechariah

OVERSHADOW

The word *overshadow* refers to how Mary became pregnant with the Christ Child (Luke 1:35). While the normal phrase for this discussion is "virgin birth," it was more accurately a virginal *conception*. (Roman Catholic tradition holds that not only was Jesus' conception miraculous, but so was His actual birth, so that Mary's virginity remained intact. This is not found in Scripture.) The Apostles' Creed says it best: "conceived by the Holy Spirit, born of the Virgin Mary."

After Gabriel announced to Mary that she would conceive and bear a son, she inquired, "How will this be, since I am a virgin?" (v. 34). It was an excellent question and it reveals that Mary had an accurate understanding of human sexuality.

Gabriel replied to Mary without really giving an answer. He said, "The Holy Spirit will come upon you, and the power of the Most High will *overshadow* you. So the holy one to be born will be called the Son of God" (v. 35). Mary would become pregnant by the Holy Spirit's "overshadowing" her. This miraculous work of the Spirit was also confirmed to Joseph: "what is conceived in her is from the Holy Spirit" (Matt. 1:20). Both Luke and Matthew confirm that Joseph was not Jesus' biological father and that Mary's pregnancy was the result of divine activity.

The word *overshadow* is used here in the New Testament (Luke 1:35) and of the cloud at the Lord's Transfiguration (Matt. 17:5; Mark 9:7; Luke 9:34). In the Old Testament it refers to God's glory covering the tabernacle: "Then the cloud covered the Tent of Meeting, and the glory of the LORD filled the tabernacle. Moses could not enter the Tent of Meeting because the cloud had settled upon it, and the glory of the LORD filled the tabernacle" (Exod. 40:34–35). By implication, the overshadowing made Mary's womb a holy place for the Son of God to dwell and protected Him from the effects of sin.

The virginal conception was how "the Word became flesh" (John 1:14). Overshadowing was the means by which the Son of God entered Mary's womb. While the word has no sexual connotations, it does indicate that the Spirit's action provided the male genetic material for the pregnancy. The incarnate Son of God received from His mother a human body and a human

– O –

nature without compromising His deity. The act of overshadowing ensured that the infant would be the "holy one" (Luke 1:35), free from the sin nature that marks every other human being. The sinlessness of the Lord Jesus Christ is taught consistently in the New Testament (2 Cor. 5:21; Heb. 4:15; 1 Pet. 2:22; 1 John 3:5). To save sinful humans, a sinless sacrifice was required (Exod. 12:5; John 1:29; 1 Pet. 1:18–19). Jesus, the perfect Son of God, is the sole, all-sufficient sacrifice for sin.

Mary's pregnancy fulfilled the prophecy of Isaiah 7:14. "The virgin will be with child and will give birth to a son, and will call him Immanuel." The writer of Hebrews, in 10:5, quotes Christ as saying "a body you prepared for me." God the Father planned the incarnation; God the Son became flesh; and the Holy Spirit of God prepared Mary's womb and the body of our Lord Jesus Christ.

♪ See: Advent, Immanuel, Jesus, Mary, Messiah, Nazarene, Virgin Birth

PATIENCE

Advent is a season of waiting. Children say, "I can't wait for Christmas to come!" But wait they must. The Jewish people waited for generations for their Messiah to come and fulfill prophecy. Not until "the time had fully come" (Gal. 4:4) was Jesus born. Waiting is often hard work but it is not wasting time or energy. The Scriptures encourage us to practice an "active waiting" that keeps us focused on Christ's return.

Why hasn't Jesus returned yet? Because God is patient, wanting sinners to find salvation (2 Pet. 3:8–9).

The only way to gain patience is to learn to wait. Not only is patience a quality that helps us handle difficult circumstances, it is a virtue when dealing with difficult people. James gives us three portraits of patience in 5:7–8, 10–11:

> Be patient, then, brothers, until the Lord's coming. See how the farmer waits for the land to yield its valuable crop and how patient he is for the autumn and spring rains. You too, be patient and stand firm, because the Lord's coming is near. . . . Brothers, as an example of patience in the face of suffering, take the prophets who spoke in the name of the Lord. As

you know, we consider blessed those who have persevered. You have heard of Job's perseverance and have seen what the Lord finally brought about. The Lord is full of compassion and mercy.

The farmer demonstrates that patience is a factor in success. Farmers wait for the weather to be right for planting. After planting, they wait for the crop to sprout and grow. Finally, they wait for harvest. Farmers do a lot of waiting but they are never doing nothing! They fertilize, deal with weeds and pests, work on machinery, and pray.

The prophets show us that patience is a mark of faithfulness. Despite opposition and abuse, Elijah, Jeremiah, and John the Baptist were faithful to proclaim the message and do the work God called them to do. Their patience proved their faith in God.

Job teaches us that patience is a sign of maturity. Job was not passive while enduring his trials: he questioned, agonized, and challenged his "comforters." Reaching maturity takes a long time. Perhaps this is the reason that it is older persons who possess patience. In Job's case, what he was waiting for was not God's gifts, but God Himself.

We are waiting for Jesus to come again. We are waiting with each other for His return. "Waiting for" is much easier when you are "waiting with."

ẻ See: Advent, Immanuel, Messiah, Prophecy, Rush

PEACE

The word *peace* in the Hebrew language is *shalom*, and it means much more than the absence of war or other disturbances. When two orthodox Jews meet, they greet each other with "Shalom," and when they depart, they also say, "Shalom." Along with peace, the word carries the ideas of health, prosperity, safety, completeness, harmony, and fulfillment. It speaks of a full and satisfying life.

We associate Christmas with peace. The priest Zechariah saw in the birth of Messiah the coming of God's light "to guide our feet into the path of peace" (Luke 1:79). But "shalom" touches death as well as life, for old Simeon prayed, "Sovereign Lord, as you have promised, you now dismiss your servant in peace" (2:29). Perhaps the most familiar "Christmas peace" statement in Scripture is the Authorized Version's translation of Luke 2:14, "Glory to God in the highest, and on earth peace, good will toward men." To enjoy Christmas peace in our own hearts and homes, we must understand four "peace announcements" found in Scripture.

The Announcement of the Angels

"Glory to God in the highest, and on earth peace, good will toward men." This translation of Luke 2:14 is a bit awkward and gives the impression that the peace Jesus brings is only for those who show "good will" to others. The New International Version reads: "Suddenly a great company of the heavenly host appeared with the angel, praising God and saying, 'Glory to God in the highest, and on earth peace to men on whom his favor rests'" (vv. 13–14). The word translated "men" is *anthropos* and means "people in general, both men and women." The angels brought their good news "for all the people" (v. 10), and yet God's peace is only for "those on whom God's favor [grace] rests." More about this later.

Before the Lord created the first man and woman, He created the angels to worship and serve Him; and some of them rebelled and were cast out of heaven (2 Pet. 2:4; Jude 6). Jesus didn't come to save the fallen angels (Heb. 2:16) but to save sinful people, and yet the angels praised God for His grace to humans! The Pax Romana (Roman Peace) had begun in AD 27, but though it brought a truce among the nations, it could not bring peace to the human heart. There has not been much "peace on earth" in recorded history and there certainly isn't much today. During the centuries, it's estimated that there has been world peace less than 10 percent of the time and that thousands of treaties have been signed and broken by national leaders.

The American poet Henry Wadsworth Longfellow lost a son in the Civil War and out of that experience he wrote a poem called "Christmas Bells." It has been set to music but is rarely sung today. Here are two selected verses that express the way many people feel about "peace on earth." We will quote another verse later.

> I heard the bells on Christmas Day
> Their old familiar carols play;
> And wild and sweet
> The words repeat
> Of peace on earth, good will to men.
>
> And in despair I bowed my head;
> "There is no peace on earth," I said;
> "For hate is strong,
> And mocks the song
> Of peace on earth, good will to men."

Were the angels wrong? Will there ever be "peace on earth"?

The Announcement of Jesus

Jesus asked, "Do you think I came to bring peace on earth?" (Luke 12:51). These are strange words from the lips of the Savior, and He had spoken them earlier, as recorded in Matthew 10:34, when He added, "I did not come to bring peace, but a sword." The statement in Matthew was part of His "commissioning sermon" when He sent His twelve disciples out to minister to the Jewish people. He wanted them to warn their converts that there was a price to pay for following Him. The Luke passage warns all believers today to be prepared for serious conflict before Jesus returns.

Jesus may be called "the Great Divider." During His ministry on earth, the people were divided over who He was and what He came to do (John 7:43; 9:16; 10:19). They could easily interpret the weather signs but not the signs of the times (Luke 12:56). God had come into their very midst and they didn't recognize Him or receive Him (19:41–44)! There are two kinds of people in the world: those who are saved because they have trusted Jesus Christ, and those who are lost, either because they have never heard the gospel or because they have heard but have rejected Christ.

There is no peace on earth. But is there any hope?

The Announcement of the Palm Sunday Crowd

"Peace in heaven and glory in the highest!" (Luke 19:38). This sounds like the announcement the angels made to the shepherds, except that this crowd declared "peace in heaven." Why? *Because heaven is the only place that knows real peace, and that's because of the finished work of Jesus on the cross!*

Why is there no peace on earth? Because people have rejected Christ and are at war with God. "What causes fights and quarrels among you? Don't they come from your desires that battle within you?" (James 4:1). People and nations are at war with one another because they are at war within themselves, and they are at war within themselves because they are at war with God. The heart of every problem is the problem in the heart (see Mark 7:17–23), and the heart is "deceitful above all things and beyond cure" (Jer. 17:9).

Let's go back to the original announcement of the angels: "Glory to God in the highest, and on earth peace to men on whom his favor rests" (Luke 2:14). This is not a prayer or a wish; it is the declaration of a fact. God doesn't save people because they have earned favor with God but because He has first revealed His grace to them in Christ and they trusted the Savior. If they already had God's favor, they would not need to be saved. This message of good news is "for all the people" (v. 10), both Jews and Gentiles (v. 32).

Because Jesus came to earth, lived a perfect life, died for our sins, rose again, and ascended to heaven, the world is reconciled to God. He could have sent Jesus to judge the world, but in His grace, He sent Jesus to save sinners (John 3:17). Through His witnessing church, He pleads with sinners to trust His Son and be reconciled to God. "All this is from God, who reconciled us to himself through Christ and gave us the ministry of reconciliation: that God was reconciling the world to himself in Christ, not counting men's sins against them. And he has committed to us the message of reconciliation" (2 Cor. 5:18–19). "Therefore, since we have been justified [declared righteous] through faith, we have peace with God through our Lord Jesus Christ" (Rom. 5:1). There is peace in the hearts and lives of believers because there is peace in heaven and the God of peace has filled us "with all joy and peace . . . by the power of the Holy Spirit" (15:13). There is peace in heaven because of God's grace, for grace and peace go together. In fact sixteen books in the New Testament open with invocations involving grace and peace.

The Announcement of the Prophet

"And he will be called . . . Prince of Peace" (Isa. 9:6). One day there shall be peace on earth when Jesus Christ, the Prince of Peace, returns and reigns in His kingdom. "Of the increase of his government and peace there will be no end" (v. 7). One day the Spirit shall be poured out from heaven and the desert will become a fertile field and there will be justice and righteousness on the earth (see Isa. 32:15–16). "The fruit of righteousness will be peace; the effect of righteousness will be quietness and confidence forever. My people will live in peaceful dwelling places, in secure homes, in undisturbed places of rest" (vv. 17–18). "They will beat their swords into plowshares and their spears into pruning hooks. Nation will not take up sword against nation, nor will they train for war anymore" (Mic. 4:3).

Meanwhile, God's people may enjoy peace on earth because peace is a fruit of the Spirit (Gal. 5:22), and if we are prayerful and thankful, the peace of God will guard our hearts and our minds (Phil. 4:6–7). "You will keep in perfect peace him whose mind is steadfast, because he trusts in you" (Isa. 26:3).

After His resurrection, Jesus greeted His disciples with, "Peace be with you!" Then He showed them the wounds in His hands and His side (John 20:19–20). Why? Because our peace with God was purchased "through his blood, shed on the cross" (Col. 1:20). But then our Lord repeated His greeting: "Peace be with you. . . . Receive the Holy Spirit" (John 20:21–22). This is the peace of God that Paul wrote about in Philippians 4:6–7, and the Lord imparts this peace as we walk in the Spirit, pray, and think on His Word.

There is no need to bow our heads in despair and be pessimistic about peace on earth. Even Longfellow knew this truth and wrote:

> Then pealed the bells more loud and deep;
> "God is not dead, nor doth He sleep!
> The wrong shall fail,
> The right prevail,
> With peace on earth, good will to men."

Longfellow was not wrong—nor were God's angels!

♪ See: Angels, Jesus, Redemption, Shepherds, Songs

PONDERING

"But Mary treasured up all these things and pondered them in her heart" (Luke 2:19).

After Jesus was born, Mary finally had time to think about all the events that resulted in her being a mother. It began with Gabriel, his appearance and his message. She said yes to God and was pregnant. There was the visit to her relative Elizabeth and her silent husband. She had told Joseph about the pregnancy, and ultimately he had believed her. The village gossips had not been convinced. Then the census was imposed, and she and Joseph had traveled to Bethlehem. After arriving, labor pains—and the birth of a son! Joy. Shepherds arrived with news that angels had informed them of the Savior's birth.

– P –

Mary's Ponderings

The word *ponder* means "to reflect on, to place together for comparison." Mary took time to be quiet and think deeply about what God had been doing in her life and her body, not only for the past nine months, but probably since she was old enough to know about God. Mary pondered, looking for meaning, identifying what was significant, and weighing the implications.

Certainly Mary thought about the wonder of it all. Why would God choose her? Who knew "overshadowing" could make her pregnant? The Messiah was to be born in Bethlehem, and a government census put them in Bethlehem for the child's birth. What of the shepherds who found their way to the manger, their tale of an angel with the announcement of the Savior's birth, and then an angelic army in the sky? The God of wonders wove all these mysteries together to bring His Son to earth, and to fulfill the ancient Scriptures.

Mary probably also pondered the identity of her child. His names Immanuel and Jesus indicated that He was more than human. Their meaning—"God with us" and "God is salvation"—pointed to Jesus' deity. How were she and Joseph to raise such a child? Could they possibly provide what He would need to become the One who would fulfill God's purpose?

Like all parents, Mary pondered the future of her child. What kind of personality would He have? Would He be aware of who He really was? If so, when? How would He get along with the rest of the family? Would He be "normal"? Could Joseph train Him to be a master carpenter?

Eventually the process of pondering had to arrive at *What am I supposed to do?* Perhaps Mary was overwhelmed at first but she was a wise woman who simply did what had to be done. Feed and change the baby. Pray for Him. Teach Him to walk and talk. Teach Him God's Word. Take Him to God's house. Pray for Him. Set a good example. Love Him. Encourage Him. Let Him grow into manhood. Challenge Him to fulfill God's call on His life. Pray for Him. When it's time, let go.

Our Need to Ponder

Determine to make time to ponder during Advent. Find a place where you can enter into silence and not be disturbed.

Ponder the mystery of the eternal Son of God entering time and space and history by being born as a helpless baby.

Ponder what it would be like to be a shepherd when the night is illumined by an angel from heaven (when has God startled you?).

Ponder being a wise man following a star (by what means has God guided you?).

Ponder the experiences that have shaped your character and life. Think about how God brought you to Himself. Think about the people God has used to bless, teach, and guide you. Can you see how God prepared you for the trials you have faced? Can you see how God used those trials to bless you? Ask yourself (and God), *Am I fulfilling God's purpose in my life?*

Ponder what God might want to change in your character. Are you willing to let God transform your perspective? What is your most valuable relationship? What is your most valuable treasure? Is there a wound that still needs to be healed?

Ponder what lies ahead. What would you like to do for God's kingdom before your life is over? Is God opening a new door for service? Who might you pour your life into spiritually? Are you willing to have your horizons broadened?

Ponder how you could help someone in need.

Ponder how you can help your family enjoy the gift of relationships this season and deemphasize the importance of presents.

Ponder what it means to you to be a child of the heavenly Father.

Pondering enables us to see the connections between "random" events. Pondering leads us to find the patterns in what God is doing. Pondering reminds us that we are part of something much bigger than ourselves. Pondering leads us to believe that God (and only God) is awesome.

In your heart, ponder.

è See: Incarnation, Mary, Overshadow, Prophecy

PROPHECY

One of the greatest Bible classes ever held on earth was taught by Jesus to two discouraged men whose world had collapsed. "And beginning with Moses and all the Prophets, he explained to them what was said in all the Scriptures concerning himself" (Luke 24:27). That included prophecies about His birth.

Philip told his friend Nathanael, "We have found the one Moses wrote about in the Law, and about whom the prophets also wrote—Jesus of Nazareth, the son of Joseph" (John 1:45).

"If you believed Moses," Jesus told the Jewish religious leaders, "you would believe me, for he wrote about me" (5:46).

Jesus is the major theme of the Old Testament, and the Christmas season is the ideal time to review what is written about His marvelous birth. What do Moses and the prophets reveal about the coming of the promised Messiah?

He would come as a human and not an angel. "And I will put enmity between you [Satan] and the woman, and between your offspring and hers; he will crush your head, and you will strike his heel" (Gen. 3:15). Jesus did not come to save fallen angels but sinful people, and therefore He needed to be human (see Heb. 2:16). He came in a truly human body, yet without sin (Luke 1:31–35; Heb. 10:5–7).

He would come as a baby and not an adult. Again the Genesis 3:15 passage speaks of the offspring of the woman. In Scripture there are demonstrated four ways to get a body: (1) without a man or a woman, as did Adam; (2) with a man but no woman, as did Eve; (3) with a man and a woman, as in normal conception and birth; and (4) with a woman but no man, as did Jesus who was conceived in Mary's virgin womb. (See Baby and Virgin Birth.)

He would come as a male and not a female. The Old Testament prophecies speak of Messiah as a man. Romans 5:12–21 explains that Adam was the head of the human race under the old creation, and 1 Timothy 2:14 explains that Adam sinned with his eyes wide open, while Eve was deceived by Satan. Jesus came as the "last Adam" to redeem the human race and establish a new creation (1 Cor. 15:20–22, 45–49; 2 Cor. 5:17).

He would come as a Jew and not a Gentile. Jesus made it clear that "salvation is from the Jews" (John 4:22). In Genesis 12:1–3 God covenanted to give Abraham many descendants and from them bless the whole world, and this blessing came through Jesus Christ (Gal. 3:16–18). Messiah would come from the tribe of Judah (Gen. 49:10; Heb. 7:14) and the family of David (2 Sam. 7:12–16), born of a virgin (Isa. 7:14; Luke 1:34–38).

He would be born in Bethlehem of Judea (Mic. 5:2; Matt. 2:1–12; Luke 2:1–20).

è See: Bethlehem, David, Genealogy, Immanuel, Jesus, King, Messiah, Nazarene

QUESTIONS

Giving the right answer is important. Most formal educational experiences teach us to value the correct answer. But the "right answer" may be overrated. Sometimes asking the right question is more important! This is the best way to gain information. Effective teachers use the "interrogative mood" to prompt students to think deeper about the topic of study. The questions we ask also reveal what's on our minds and hearts.

The Bible is full of questions, some asked by God (see Job 38–41), some by key Bible characters, others by the psalmists, the prophets, the apostles, and even the Lord Jesus.

The seasons of Advent and Christmas prompt children to ask all sorts of questions. Why are there lights on so many houses now? Where did we get this Christmas tree ornament? When can we start listening to Christmas music? Is Santa real? Do we have to eat lutefisk at Grandma's house? Who will wrap the gifts? How much nutmeg goes into the Yule bread? What does a candy cane represent?

Journalists-in-training learn the six basic interrogatives: Who? What? When? Where? Why? How? Each of these interrogatives appears in Scripture, but the Advent and Christmas texts contain only three questions.

Zechariah's Question

Zechariah asked the first question in the infancy narratives, responding to the angel Gabriel's message that Zechariah and Elizabeth would have a baby son. His question was: "How can I be sure of this?" He hastened to add his reason for asking: "I am an old man and my wife is well along in years" (Luke 1:18).

Perhaps Zechariah had waited so long to become a father that he had reached the point where he was convinced it wouldn't happen. Maybe he felt he was a realist and was preventing himself from getting his hopes up only to be disappointed. His question might also be interpreted as "Are you sure you've got the right man?"

Gabriel's response and Zechariah's subsequent silence tell us that his question was born of doubt. God, through Gabriel, had given His plan and promise; Zechariah's question put a shadow over the good news. God knows our hearts, what we truly think and believe. Zechariah was focused on himself and missed the potency and joy of God's message.

When God speaks to us, our response reveals the condition of our heart. Zechariah was a priest who served in the temple, who encountered an angel of God, yet he struggled to believe what God said.

Where do you struggle to believe God's word to you? Are you skeptical of God's promises? Do you feel God owes you an explanation or has to provide proof before you'll obey?

Still, God kept His word to Zechariah. Elizabeth became pregnant, and somehow Zechariah communicated the story of his angelic encounter to Elizabeth. They agreed on the name John, even though it wasn't in the family. Zechariah had nine months to silently ponder God's message, the state of his heart, and what would happen in the days ahead. When his son, John, was born, Zechariah sang a sweet song of salvation, full of Scripture and praise and faith in God.

– Q –

Mary's Question

Mary raises the second question in the infancy narratives. She, too, is responding to a message from the angel Gabriel, who has informed her that she will be the human mother of Jesus, Messiah, God's Son. Her question, "How will this be, since I am a virgin?" (Luke 1:34), reveals her moral and sexual purity. She knew how children were conceived and she knew she was a virgin.

Mary's question is born of faith in God. She knew that Adam and Eve had been created apart from sexual union. She believed God could bypass the normal manner of conception if He chose to. She was not questioning God's sovereignty over her life and body, nor was she demanding an explanation. She was curious about the "how" (and maybe wondering why God was bypassing marriage). God's method of producing this pregnancy was the overshadowing work of the Holy Spirit (v. 35). Probably this answer didn't fully answer her question, but the result was that the Christ Child was conceived in Mary's womb and she carried Him until His birth.

Gabriel did provide insight into why God chose virginal conception as the means of the incarnation. He said, "the holy one to be born will be called the Son of God." In His overshadowing ministry, the Holy Spirit prevented Jesus from receiving a sin nature. The result was a God-Man, untainted by sin, who would live a perfect life and be qualified to be the substitutionary sacrifice for the sin of all people.

It is not wrong to ask questions of God, provided the question is asked with the right motive and attitude. God is not obligated to give an answer. In Mary's case, she did receive answers, but they made clear sense only later. What questions do you have as God is shaping your life? Go ahead and ask but don't demand. Look to Scripture for answers. Expect that God's answers may be only sufficient to lead you to the next step. God rarely tells us what He's doing ahead of time.

The Wise Men's Question

The wise men made the final inquiry in the infancy narratives. Having followed the Messiah's star as far as Jerusalem, and expecting that everyone there would be aware of the new king's birth, they asked, "Where is the one who has been born king of the Jews?" (Matt. 2:2). Probably the Magi asked the citizens and shopkeepers, as they entered the city, and the priests and Levites outside the temple. Eventually the question reached Herod, who was surprised because he assumed that *he* was the king of the Jews! Here are visitors in town who know more about what's going on than the locals do! Herod was disturbed by this question, and the people of Jerusalem were disturbed because Herod was disturbed.

The theological experts reported that Messiah would be born in Bethlehem (Mic. 5:2; Matt. 2:6). The Magi found the Christ Child there and worshiped Him. They returned home without reporting to Herod, because God so directed them through a dream (v. 12).

We should not be surprised when leaders and rulers are threatened by the claim of Jesus to be King. Throughout history many governments have tried to suppress Christianity because they want the citizens' highest loyalty to be to the state. This explains much of the persecution that Christians endure around the globe today. The question, at least in a political discussion, is not so much "Where is the king?" as it is "WHO is the king?" Herod tried to ensure he was the only king by having all the infant boys in Bethlehem killed (vv. 16–18). Herod was an Edomite and knew he could not rightly claim the throne of David. The newborn King, however, was of David's line.

Where is King Jesus? Not in the capital city. Not in the temple. He is not with the rich and powerful. He is with the poor and ordinary and obscure. Where is King Jesus? He should be reigning in His Church. Where is King Jesus? He should be on the throne of our hearts and at the center of our homes and marriages.

– Q –

Sometimes a simple question can generate conflict. A child asks, "Why don't we go to church?" and parents feel guilty. A spouse asks, "When can we pray together?" and the partner is embarrassed. A pastor asks the congregation, "Where are you putting your financial resources?" and church members get defensive. A parent asks her teenager, "How will going to that movie reflect on your relationship with Jesus?" An accountant asks a business owner, "Do you realize the consequences of failing to report that income?" A Christian friend asks, "Are you ready to trust Jesus as your Savior?"

What questions are you asking? What questions are being asked of you?

℮ See: Herod the Great, King, Mary, Overshadow, Virgin Birth, Wise Men, Zechariah

REDEMPTION

Freedom is a gift that oppressed people long for. Freedom is a treasure that its possessors must never take for granted. When Zechariah prophesied in song, his opening words were "Praise be to the Lord, the God of Israel, because he has come and has redeemed his people" (Luke 1:68). The word *redeem* means "to pay a price to set someone free." Zechariah sang a song of redemption!

Redeem was a familiar word at the time of Christ's birth. The Roman Empire had perhaps as many as sixty million slaves, and some slaves were fortunate enough to purchase their freedom. Prisoners of war were sometimes liberated by being exchanged for prisoners on the other side; sometimes prisoners of war were freed because their king paid a ransom. In both examples, freedom was gained because a price was paid.

Jesus came to redeem sinners from their sin. Human beings are sinful by nature and there is no way a sinner can escape the power and consequences of sin by himself. We are born slaves to sin (Rom. 7:14). The incarnation was a rescue mission to break our spiritual chains.

The paradox in this rescue mission is that Jesus accepted limitations to liberate us. "But when the time had fully come, God sent his Son, born of a woman, born under law, to redeem those under law" (Gal. 4:4). Jesus took on the limitations of time and space, a human body, and the demands of God's law.

His sinless life qualified Him to be our substitute by dying on the cross for our sin. "In him we have redemption through his blood" (Eph. 1:7). The price of our spiritual redemption was Christ's shed blood. The writer to the Hebrews says that Christ "died as a ransom" to set us free (Heb. 9:15). Our redemption is not something we deserved—it is provided by God's grace: we "are justified freely by his grace through the redemption that came by Christ Jesus" (Rom. 3:24). The price of our redemption cannot be measured.

Our spiritual freedom in Christ has two dimensions. First, there is *freedom from*. Jesus sets us free from the power of sin and Satan, from the penalty of sin, from the guilt of sin, and from the fear of punishment. As we mature in our faith, Jesus will continue to set us free from wrong thinking, from past wounds, and from habits that stunt our growth.

The other dimension is that Jesus redeems us so that we are *free to*. Because of our new relationship to God and the indwelling Holy Spirit, we are free to obey God's commands, to love God and others, to forgive those who have hurt us, and to serve others in the name of Christ. We are free to grow into the person Christ intends us to be. We are free to draw on the spiritual wealth that is ours in Christ.

But freedom must not be abused! The apostle Paul cautioned the Galatian believers, "You, my brothers, were called to be free. But do not use your freedom to indulge the sinful nature; rather, serve one another in love" (Gal. 5:13). Redemption does not mean the right to do as I please. It means Christ set me free to do what is right, and that means serving others. Freedom is best enjoyed and appreciated when we use it responsibly and gratefully.

Are you in bondage in some area of your life? Are you tired enough of it to submit yourself to Jesus and let Him redeem you? This is the greatest paradox of spiritual freedom: we are free only when we surrender completely to Jesus.

❦ See: Immanuel, Jesus, Prophecy, World

RUSH

Luke wrote of the shepherds who heard the angel's message, "So they hurried off [literally 'came hastening'] and found Mary and Joseph, and the baby, who was lying in the manger" (Luke 2:16). This has been called "the first Christmas rush," but in today's competitive commercial society, the "Christmas rush" isn't that spiritual. Most of the people involved aren't looking for Jesus. That would be a distraction. It's more of a desperate, last-minute attempt to find gifts for the people whose names are still on the shopping list. There is so much to do during the Christmas season that some people postpone their shopping until almost the last minute, perhaps hoping to find bargains.

The word translated "found" literally means "to find after searching." The wise men had a star to guide them to the house (Matt. 2:9), but the shepherds had to search until they found a baby wrapped in cloths and lying in a feeding trough (Luke 2:12). It was worth it! They weren't looking for a last-minute gift to purchase but for an eternal Gift to receive, the greatest Gift of all. No wonder the shepherds glorified and praised God and told everybody about the Baby!

❦ See: Patience, Pondering, Shepherds

SHEPHERDS

In the same region there were some shepherds staying out in the fields and keeping watch over their flock by night. And an angel of the Lord suddenly stood before them, and the glory of the Lord shone around them; and they were terribly frightened. But the angel said to them, "Do not be afraid; for behold, I bring you good news of great joy which will be for all the people; for today in the city of David there has been born for you a Savior, who is Christ the Lord. This will be a sign for you: you will find a baby wrapped in cloths and lying in a manger." And suddenly there appeared with the angel a multitude of the heavenly host praising God and saying, "Glory to God in the highest, and on earth peace among men with whom He is pleased." . . . So they came in a hurry and found their way to Mary and Joseph, and the baby as He lay in the manger.

Luke 2:8–14, 16 NASB

It was just another night shift with the flocks outside of Bethlehem. The shepherds expected the normal routine. Then the sky lit up with heaven's glory, an angel delivered news of the Savior's birth, and an angelic choir presented a celestial concert.

We don't know the name of a single shepherd. But they were important to God. What can we learn from the shepherds? By the nature of their work, shepherds were considered "unclean," which meant they could not go to worship at the temple. Shepherds were not permitted to testify as witnesses in court either. So those whose lives were devoted to keeping the law looked down on them. That's strange when you consider that Abraham and Moses and David were shepherds. When His Son was born, God communicated not with the rulers in Jerusalem but with hardworking shepherds. God's presence and grace came to them through the angels. The shepherds' response was to go and see the infant Savior, and then they became witnesses of His birth. *So the shepherds tell us of the goodness of God.*

Bethlehem's hills had provided sheep pasture for centuries, but there was nothing especially attractive about the place. Then one bright angel broke into the sky above the shepherds, and then a heavenly host. Light dispelled the darkness. The shepherds got to see what is usually invisible to human eyes. They were afraid, but the angel told them not to fear. God was a lot closer than the shepherds knew! They didn't have to go to the temple in Jerusalem to find God; He found them. *The shepherds remind us of the nearness of God.*

The angel explained to the shepherds the kind of gift God had sent to the world. It was a gift "for all the people," not just for the Jewish people. It was the gift of a person, a person who would become the Savior of the world. *The shepherds teach us something about the thoughtfulness of God.* He gave what the world needed. The name Jesus means "God is salvation," or "Jehovah saves." The name Immanuel means "God is with us."

God chose the shepherds specifically to hear first of the Savior's birth, because they represented the vocation that His Son would pursue: He is the Good Shepherd (John 10:11, 14). The sheep on the Bethlehem hillside were probably destined to be sacrificed in the temple. Jesus, the Lamb of God, came to be the final, all-sufficient sacrifice to take away the sin of the world (1:29). *The shepherds point to the faithfulness of God, who kept His promise to send a Savior.* Did the shepherds look at baby Jesus and see the Lamb of God or the Good Shepherd? We don't know. They left the manger and returned to the same job, but they were changed persons.

The shepherds could have focused on the experience of seeing angels and hearing the good news. Instead, they took action. They believed the angel, searched for and found the child (a baby in a manger, most unusual), and then became witnesses of what God had done. The purpose of a spiritual experience is to equip us to do and say something for God.

  ❧ See: **Bethlehem, Inn, Light, Manger, Mary, Opportunity, Peace, Pondering**

SIMEON

Tradition holds that Simeon was an old man when he met Joseph, Mary, and Jesus in the temple (Luke 2:25–35). But it is just that—tradition. Because he had been told he would not die until he saw the Lord's Messiah, scholars assume that Simeon had a long life. He may have lived into old age, but we don't know for certain.

Simeon was a man in tune with the Holy Spirit, a rare thing before the Day of Pentecost. The Spirit's work in Simeon's life is seen in his character—"righteous and devout" (v. 25). Living in Jerusalem, Simeon probably was regularly at the temple to worship and hear the Scriptures. His words of praise to God and prophecy to Mary reveal a mind and heart saturated with God's Word. As the author of Scripture, the Holy Spirit uses the Word of God to shape our minds, hearts, and wills. By some means that Simeon clearly understood, the Holy Spirit revealed to him that prior to his dying he would see, with his own two eyes, the Messiah (v. 26). This insight into God's plan made Simeon a man who lived with a sense of great anticipation! He was also a patient man as he waited for the "consolation of Israel" (v. 25).

Simeon must have done a lot of thinking about the Messiah. Did he initially expect to meet a grown man, perhaps a military leader, or a priest? When did Simeon perceive that the Messiah might still be a child when he saw Him? Certainly Simeon meditated on what seeing the Messiah would mean to him personally, to Israel, to the Gentile nations, and to the Messiah's parents. His words (spoken or sung) in response to holding the infant Jesus reveal a familiarity with Scripture that has grasped the depths of God's saving work. His words are well-crafted poetry, expressing the fulfillment of his heart's desire and his celebration of the saving work that Jesus would do.

Led by the Holy Spirit, Simeon came to the temple at just the right moment to meet Joseph, Mary, and Jesus. How did Simeon know that Jesus was the One? Perhaps he had overheard Mary or Joseph call the infant by His name Jesus. Simeon was focused on God's salvation (v. 30), and *Jesus* means "God is salvation," or "Jehovah saves." More likely, though, the Holy Spirit prompted him to approach the little family.

Perhaps Simeon saw them offering their sacrifice of doves or pigeons in the temple (vv. 23–24). Evidently he was not disappointed that they were an ordinary-looking and poor family. Did he ask permission to hold the baby or did he just walk right up and scoop baby Jesus into his arms? Imagine the love and joy and relief Simeon felt as he cradled the Messiah. What did Joseph and Mary think or say? What parents wouldn't be startled and concerned if a stranger approached, picked up their newborn child, and began talking to God? But when Mary and Joseph heard his words, they marveled at what he said about Jesus (v. 33).

Let's consider more closely Simeon's carefully prepared and beautifully expressed words in Luke 2:29–32:

> Sovereign Lord, as you have promised,
>   you now dismiss your servant in peace.
> For my eyes have seen your salvation,
>   which you have prepared in the sight of all people,

> a light for revelation to the Gentiles
> and for glory to your people Israel.

The "song" begins as an *anthem of praise*, celebrating the Sovereign Lord who fulfills His promises and blesses His servants. Then it becomes a *gospel song*, emphasizing the salvation God has provided through His Son, the Messiah. The final stanza is a *missionary march*, offering God's salvation to both Gentiles and Jews.

Simeon blessed Joseph and Mary (v. 34a). What did he say? Did he quote the priestly blessing from Numbers 6:24–26? Possibly he offered his own blessing; Simeon was good with words. Joseph and Mary were grateful for his good and godly words spoken to and for them (and were probably no longer nervous about this strange man!).

Before he left them, Simeon spoke prophetic words to Mary: "This child is destined to cause the falling and rising of many in Israel, and to be a sign that will be spoken against, so that the thoughts of many hearts will be revealed. And a sword will pierce your own soul too" (Luke 2:34–35).

Simeon's life is worth imitating. He lived according to God's truth, led by God's Spirit. He knew how to wait actively, anticipating the moment when God would keep His promise. He had just the right words for the moment of Messiah's arrival, and he had wisdom to help Mary understand her role. Simeon lived his life for Christ and he understood the implications of Jesus' life and death. Although Simeon met the Messiah for only a brief moment, it was enough. Simeon was satisfied by the goodness, the faithfulness, and the salvation of God in Christ.

è See: Anna, Holy Spirit, Joy, Light, Mary, Messiah, Songs

SONGS

The birth of Jesus Christ has been marked from the beginning by joyful praise to the Lord, and the tradition continues today.

From Handel's *Messiah* to the latest popular tune, the Christmas season moves along on music. However, not every song you hear gives glory to the Lord as do the songs that Dr. Luke recorded in his Gospel. None of the other Gospel writers mention any of these five songs that Luke gives us. Each song is distinctive and reflects the special joys of the singers.

Elizabeth: "Bless the Lord!"

As the wife of Zechariah and the mother of John the Baptist, Elizabeth had much for which to give thanks (Luke 1:41–45). As a woman past the age of bearing children, she was sharing in a miracle from the Lord and was going to bear a famous son. When she heard Mary's greeting, she was filled with the Spirit and the baby leaped in her womb. She rejoiced at God's grace and the way He had blessed Mary "among women" (not "above" women) for the Son God had given her, and for the faith He gave her to believe His Word and obey it. It was all of grace! Elizabeth's focus was on the Lord, a good example for us to follow as we celebrate His birth each year.

Mary: "Magnify the Lord!"

Mary's song is called the Magnificat, from the Latin version of the New Testament ("My soul doth magnify the Lord" in KJV; translated "glorifies" in NIV) (Luke 1:46–56). She is not ashamed to say that the Lord is her Savior, and she begins with personal rejoicing because of the great things He has done for her (vv. 46–49). She had given her body to the Lord (v. 38; see Rom. 12:1), and now her soul and spirit were rejoicing. First the sacrifice and then the singing was the pattern in the Old Testament (1 Chron. 29:27).

Mary knew that all generations would bless her, not for herself but for what God had done for her and through her. It was God's mercy and not her merit that brought her this honor, and that mercy is extended to all who trust Him. In verses 50–53,

Mary rejoices because the Lord in His grace has turned things upside down. He scatters the proud, dethrones the mighty, and promotes the humble! He feeds the poor and sends the rich away hungry! This is the grace of God through Jesus Christ. In verses 54–55 Mary praises God for His faithfulness to His covenant promises to Israel, for her Son would have a ministry to Israel as well as to the Gentiles (Rom. 15:8–13).

Zechariah: The Theology of Christmas

You would expect an experienced priest to be a theologian and to see in these remarkable events the blessings God was giving to Israel. Like Elizabeth and Mary, Zechariah was filled with the Spirit as he praised God for His mighty works on behalf of the nation (Luke 1:67–79). The coming of God's Son to earth meant redemption and salvation, the setting free of a people in bondage. Though the Jews wanted political freedom and the restoration of David's kingdom, spiritual freedom was far more important (vv. 68–75). One day Israel would enjoy kingdom blessings, but first, Messiah had to bring salvation. The last half of Zechariah's song focuses on the ministry of his son, John, as he would prepare the way for the Savior (vv. 76–79). Zechariah saw in these events the dawning of a new day for people living in darkness and the fear of death. "Joy to the world, the Lord is come!"

The Angels: Glory and Grace

When one angel appeared in glory, it frightened the shepherds; but when an army of angels suddenly appeared and glorified God for His grace, the shepherds believed and went to search for the newborn King (Luke 2:13–14). In His birth Jesus brought many blessings to us, but the main reason for His coming was to glorify God through the salvation of those "on whom his favor [grace] rests." "For it is by grace you have been saved, through faith—and this not from yourselves, it is the gift of God" (Eph. 2:8). Three times in Ephesians 1, Paul tells us that God saved us "to the praise of his glorious grace" (vv. 6, 12, 14). God's grace and God's glory always go together. Armies usually announce war, but the angelic army (host) announced peace. That is something to sing about!

Simeon: "Do You See What I See?"

We assume that Simeon was an elderly man, for he was looking forward to the time when God would call him home. He belonged to that faithful Jewish remnant that believed the Scriptures, prayed faithfully, and looked longingly for the promised Messiah to come. Then one day Simeon entered the temple and saw the Messiah! (Luke 2:28–32). "For my eyes have seen your salvation" (v. 30). The name Jesus means "Jehovah is salvation." But Simeon also saw a throne, for he addressed God as "Sovereign Lord." The English word *despot* comes from the Greek word translated "Sovereign." Simeon saw in Jesus the hope of the world, for this gracious salvation was for all people (vv. 30–31). He saw that the "dividing wall of hostility" between Jews and Gentiles would be broken down and that believing Jews and Gentiles would be one body in Jesus Christ (Eph. 2:14–18). Finally, he saw that the glory of God that had once dwelt with Israel had now returned to God's people Israel in the person of Jesus Christ (Rom. 9:1–5).

That's a great deal to see at Christmas! If we want a truly blessed Christmas, we must see what Simeon saw.

𝕖 See: Angels, Elizabeth, Glory, Mary, Simeon, Zechariah

STAR

Jesus was born in very humble circumstances, and yet each of the kingdoms in God's great creation honored Him. The animals welcomed Him into their stable and gave Him a food trough for a bed. The vegetable kingdom was represented by the gifts of frankincense and myrrh, both derived from plants. The mineral kingdom gave up its gold, and shepherds and wise men represented the human kingdom. From the highest heavens the angels came, and from the planetary heavens His star appeared in the east. All creation worshiped the Creator.

For centuries, astronomers have been studying and debating as they have attempted to identify the remarkable star. Some suggest it was the conjunction of two planets, perhaps Jupiter and Saturn; but the Greek word (*aster*) signifies one star and not a group of stars (*astron*). Others think it was a super nova that exploded and then faded away. But planets and novae aren't low enough in the heavens to guide travelers to a specific place, and they don't move in that fashion. We have to conclude that "his star" (Matt. 2:2) was a miracle of God, a special star assigned to lead the Gentile visitors to Jesus.

The scenario was probably like this. In ancient times people believed that the birth of great men was announced by the stars. These astrologer-priests saw the new star appear in the east and concluded from their studies that it announced the birth of a Jewish king. The logical place to find this king would be in Jerusalem, so they began their journey to Judea and, knowing the route, they didn't need the star to guide them. Arriving in Jerusalem, they learned that the King would be born in Bethlehem, only six miles away. As they left, they saw the star again and it led them to the very house where Jesus, Mary, and Joseph were staying. Warned by God, the wise men took another route home.

God leads people in ways they can understand. The Law of Moses forbade the Jews from meddling with astrology and signs in the heavens, so God spoke to the Jews through His Word (Mic. 5:2); but He used a star to get the attention of the Gentiles. The wise men didn't stop with seeing the star but pressed on until they found the Savior. The traditional liturgical calendar of the Christian Church assigns January 6 as the date to commemorate this occasion of the Gentiles coming to honor the Savior. It's called Epiphany, which means "manifestation."

ɛ See: Epiphany, Herod the Great, Wise Men

TEARS

Most of us associate Christmas with joy, and rightly so; but we must remember that there are people for whom Christmas also means sorrow and tears. On more than one occasion we have been called on to conduct funerals during the Christmas season, and sometimes it was a child whose funeral we were conducting. When the Christmas season arrives, memories of departed loved ones can bring pain even in the midst of joy.

The birth of Jesus is associated with sorrow, for in his attempt to destroy Jesus, King Herod the Great killed all the boys in Bethlehem who were two years old and under (Matt. 2:16–18). Bethlehem was not a big city and perhaps no more than twenty boys were brutally slain, but even one is too many. Imagine the sorrow of the people in that little town! During his cruel reign, Herod had killed three of his own sons, so it was no problem for him to kill the sons of other people. He sired an evil family, for his son Herod Antipas killed John the Baptist (Matthew 14), and his grandson Herod Agrippa I killed the apostle James and tried to kill Peter (Acts 12).

The Christmas narrative in Luke's Gospel is saturated with joy, but Matthew introduces tragedy into the story. Why would God permit innocent little boys to be slain, and why did Matthew record this event?

For one thing, Matthew's account reminds us that the coming of Jesus into this world was a declaration of war. (Read Luke 11:14–26.) Throughout Old Testament history, Satan had tried to destroy the nation of Israel, especially the family of David, and thereby prevent the Savior from being born. At one point, wicked Queen Athaliah had all the royal sons slain and only Jehoash (Joash) escaped to carry on the Davidic line (2 Chron. 22:10–23:21). Satan tried to destroy Jesus after He was born but never succeeded. Today Satan attacks God's people, the Church. There were more martyrs for the faith in the twentieth century than in all the preceding centuries! The Christian life is not a playground; it's a battleground, and we must be armed and alert (Eph. 6:10–18; 1 Pet. 5:8–11).

But Matthew saw more than a battle in the death of the children. He connected the event with an Old Testament mother, Rachel, and an Old Testament prophet, Jeremiah. When Jacob was returning home to Bethel, his favorite wife Rachel died near Bethlehem while giving birth to a son (Gen. 35:16–20; 48:7). In her pain, she named the boy Ben-Oni, which means "son of my trouble," but by faith Jacob changed the name to Benjamin, "son of my right hand." The Jews honored Rachel's name and remembered that she died near Bethlehem.

When the Babylonians overpowered Judah, they took more than ten thousand captives to Babylon (2 Kings 24:8–17), and one of the towns on their journey was Ramah in the tribe of Benjamin. In Jeremiah 31:15–17, Jeremiah pictured Rachel, the mother of Benjamin, weeping over her children going into captivity. It was as though her own death in bringing Benjamin into the world was a futile sacrifice. She had previously given birth to Joseph, and now the tribes were in captivity to Babylon. But just as Jacob by faith had changed his son's name from "son of my trouble" to "son of my right hand," so Jeremiah by faith looked into the future and saw the nation released and restored to their land after seventy years (25:1, 11–12). Their tears would be turned into songs of joy (31:11–13; 33:10–11)!

Today we associate Bethlehem with the joyful birth of Jesus, not the death of Rachel or the captivity of the Jews. Yes, Jesus was "a man of sorrows and familiar with suffering" (Isa. 53:3), but He is also the glorified Son at the Father's right hand (Mark 16:19; Acts 2:33–34; Eph. 1:20). He is Benjamin, not Ben-Oni!

Do you have tears at Christmas? Is your name "son of trouble"? For the Christian believer, Bethlehem is not a place of death but a place of birth, the birth of Jesus Christ the Son of God. He has conquered death "and has brought life and immortality to light through the gospel" (2 Tim. 1:10). "'So there is hope for your future,' declares the LORD" (Jer. 31:17), for Jesus Christ is our hope (1 Tim. 1:1). "Weeping may remain for a night, but rejoicing comes in the morning" (Ps. 30:5).

❧ See: Bethlehem, Innocents, Mary

TIDINGS

The statement of the angel to the shepherds "I bring you good tidings of great joy" (Luke 2:10 KJV) is a familiar part of our Christmas celebration, even though the word *tidings* isn't commonly used in conversation today. It comes from an Old English word that means "to happen," so *tidings* means "news of an event." The Authorized Version uses "tidings" forty-five times, and faithful Bible readers will especially recall Isaiah 52:7, "How beautiful upon the mountains are the feet of him that bringeth good tidings, that publisheth peace."

In the original Greek text of Luke's Gospel, the word translated "I bring . . . good news" is *euangelizo* and gives us our word *evangelize*, which means "to tell the good news." In his translation of the New Testament, John Wycliffe translated Luke 2:10, "I evangelize to you a great joy." Ken Taylor's *Living Gospels* reads, "I bring you the most joyful news ever announced, and it is for everyone!" Gabriel used the same word when he spoke to Zechariah the priest, "I have been sent . . . to tell you this good news" (1:19). The noted British preacher Charles Haddon Spurgeon called the angel who spoke to the shepherds "the first evangelist under the gospel dispensation."

Tidings can be either bad or good, and the tidings of the birth of Jesus are superlatively good. A Savior has been born! The true joy of Christmas is the joy of those who have trusted Jesus Christ and received God's loving gift of salvation (Eph. 2:8–9). It isn't enough to believe that God loved the world and sent His Son (John 3:16) or that Christ loved the church and died for it (Eph. 5:25). We must be able to say with Paul, "the Son of God . . . loved me and gave himself for me" (Gal. 2:20).

It would be great if tomorrow's newspaper headlines announced, "Cure discovered for cancer and AIDS!" That would make millions of sick people very happy and even more healthy people very relieved. But the good news of Christmas is even greater, for "the Father has sent his Son to be the Savior of the world" (1 John 4:14). These glad tidings are for you!

𝄞 See: Greetings, Joy, Shepherds, Zechariah

"UNTO US"

Group gifts are not always enjoyable. A family we know got a new jigsaw puzzle each year at Christmas. Some family members loved to work on puzzles and would sit at the table for hours getting the pieces to fit. But several other family members disliked puzzles intensely and refused to participate. Some gifts are intended for everyone in the family or office group, but often not every individual appreciates the gift.

Jesus came to earth as God's gift for everyone—the group gift that can be appreciated by every person. Isaiah wrote, "For *unto us* a child is born, *unto us* a son is given: and the government shall be upon his shoulder: and his name shall be called Wonderful, Counsellor, The mighty God, The everlasting Father, The Prince of Peace" (Isa. 9:6 KJV). Who is "us"? Initially, it was the people of Israel. But it was always God's plan to bring salvation to all the peoples of the world through the nation of Israel.

On the night Christ was born, the angel said to the shepherds, "For *unto you* is born this day in the city of David a Saviour, which is Christ the Lord" (Luke 2:11 KJV). The "you" was the shepherds, who were Jews; and the "you" was the Jewish nation. But the angel had also said, "I bring you good news of great joy that will be for all the *people*" (v. 10). We find the word *people* in the phrase "people of God." In the Old Testament "the people" or "my people" refers to the Jews (Exod. 5:1). But in the New Testament the phrase "people of God" means those persons who belong to God's family through saving faith in Jesus Christ (see Acts 15:14—"how God at first showed his concern by taking from the Gentiles a people for himself"; see also Titus 2:14, 1 Pet. 2:9–10).

Jesus came to the world for God's chosen people, Israel; He is their Messiah. But He also came for the "other sheep" (John 10:16), the Gentiles who would join the Jews in making up the Church (Rom. 9:24–25; Eph. 2:11–18). Jesus came for the sake of every ethnic group and every person.

Is there someone you don't want to have the gift of salvation? Those we consider enemies are usually people we want to punish. In today's world some Christians don't want to share the gospel with terrorists or criminals or those who are in any way different from them. But God put no restrictions on His gift of Jesus; neither should we.

"Unto us" a child is born—unto Jews, Gentiles, the human race, the whole world of people. "Unto you" is born a Savior—unto you personally.

What will you do with God's gift?

ὲ See: Gifts, Redemption, Songs, Tidings

VIRGIN BIRTH

When Joseph discovered that Mary, his betrothed, was with child, he didn't know what to do. He believed she was a virgin, and it wasn't possible for a virgin to be pregnant, and she certainly had not been unfaithful to him. The Lord revealed to Joseph that her child was the promised Messiah, the Son of God (Matt. 1:18–25). The phrase "virgin birth" refers to this miraculous event and informs us that Jesus came into the world having a human mother who bore Him but not a human father who had begotten Him (v. 16; Luke 1:26–56). Joseph was His father only according to the law, but he had no part in the conception of Jesus in Mary's womb. This was accomplished by the Holy Spirit (v. 35).

Is the doctrine of the virgin birth significant? It certainly is, for it involves three very important matters that affect every Christian believer.

The Authority of the Word of God

The first important matter is the authority of the Word of God. Beginning with Genesis 3:15, which is the first promise of the Savior in Scripture, the major theme of the Old Testament is that the Savior is coming (Luke 24:25–27, 44–45; and see Prophecy). The law God gave to the Jews was to protect the nation and keep it separated from moral and spiritual pollution so it could be a channel through which God could send His Son. Isaiah 7:14 affirms that the Savior would be born of a virgin, and if that prophecy is not true, can we trust any other portion of the Scripture? Matthew and Luke mention the virgin birth in the very first chapters of their Gospels. If they lied about the birth of Christ, can we trust what they wrote about His life, miracles, teachings, crucifixion, resurrection, and ascension?

The Deity of Jesus Christ

The second important matter is the deity of Jesus Christ. If Jesus is the Son of God—and He is—then He existed before the creation of the universe *and before His mother.* The Holy Spirit conceived the Son in Mary's womb, and the angel Gabriel told her that "the holy one to be born will be called the Son of God" (Luke 1:35). Isaiah 9:6 says, "For to us a child is born [the humanity of Jesus], to us a son is given" [the deity of Jesus]. Jesus Himself taught that He "came down from heaven" and was "sent by the Father" (John 5:23–24, 30, 38–40; 6:32–33, 38, 41–42, 50–51, 58; 16:28; and see 17:5, 24). Each baby born into this world is a new individual that has never existed before. Jesus existed with the Father and the Spirit from eternity (1:1–4).

The Reality of Salvation

Third, the virgin birth is important for the reality of salvation. If Jesus is not the perfect Lamb of God, how could He effectively offer Himself on the cross as the sacrifice for the sins of the world (John 1:29; 1 Pet. 2:24)? "Can any of you prove me guilty of sin?" Jesus asked some of His enemies (John 8:46). He had no sin (2 Cor. 5:21), He was without sin (Heb. 4:15; 7:26), and He committed no sin (1 Pet. 2:22; 1 John 3:5). Had He been conceived as any other baby, He would have had a sinful nature (Ps. 51:5); but He was conceived by the Holy Spirit and therefore sinless.

  ❦ See: Immanuel, Incarnation, Mary, Messiah, Overshadow, Prophecy

WISE MEN

If we are to understand the importance of the wise men in the Christmas narrative, we must first sweep away the traditional debris that has cluttered their story and obscured the true facts.

Contrary to the lyrics of a popular Christmas song, these men were not "three kings." They were priest-scientists who studied the heavens. (The tradition about kings may have arisen from Psalm 72:10–11 and Isaiah 60:1–11.) The Greek word in Matthew 2:1, 7, and 16 is *magos* and refers to "scientists" or "wise men" in the ancient world. In the book of Daniel, it is the title of the men who interpreted dreams; the NIV translates the word "astrologers" (2:2, 4–5, 10; 4:7; 5:7, 11). The Jewish people were forbidden to practice divination (Deut. 18:10–13; Jer. 10:1–2; see Isa. 47:13–14), but these visitors were Gentiles who probably came from Persia. They had seen a remarkable new star in the heavens and had interpreted it to mean that a Jewish king had been born. The logical place to find a Jewish king would be in Jerusalem, so that's where they headed. During their time in exile, the Jewish scribes may have taught the

Babylonian and Persian scholars about the Messianic promises. Some students point to Numbers 24:17 as a possible connection.

We do not know how many Magi were in the group and we do not know their names. The fact that three gifts are mentioned has led people to think that three men were involved, but that conclusion could be wrong. The word *treasures* can mean "treasure chests" (the Greek gives us our word *thesaurus*), suggesting many more than three gifts. These wise men certainly did not make that long trip alone but were part of a large camel train of servants and soldiers and supplies. If three strangers showed up in Jerusalem, it wouldn't make much of a stir; but when a large and rich-looking foreign company appeared, everybody took notice, especially King Herod.

In spite of what we see in manger sets and "living Christmas" displays, the wise men did not come to the manger but to a house in Bethlehem. They did not see a newborn baby in a feeding trough but a young child, probably in His mother's arms (Matt. 2:9–12). Among the Jews, as soon as children completed one year of life, they were considered to be two years old. Note that, when referring to the family, Matthew always mentioned Jesus, "the child," first (Matt. 2:11, 13–14, 20–21).

So much for the historical facts. Now let's consider the spiritual truths behind these facts.

To begin with, the coming of the Magi shows God's concern for Gentiles as well as Jews. Jesus is indeed "the Savior of the world" (John 4:42; 1 John 4:14), and there are "other sheep" He wants us to help reach that are not in the Jewish fold (John 10:16). The visit of the Magi to Jesus is commemorated on the church calendar on January 6 and is called Epiphany. The word means "revelation" or "manifestation" and refers to Christ being revealed to the Gentiles. The gospel message was proclaimed by Peter first to the Jews (Acts 2–7), then to the Samaritans (Acts 8), and then to the Gentiles (Acts 10), and then Paul took the message to both Jews and Gentiles throughout the Roman empire. God loves the world and wants to see all nations come to salvation (Matt. 28:19–20).

– W –

Second, God reveals Himself to people in ways they can understand. In the case of the Magi, the Lord revealed Himself first through nature when He revealed that special star. They decided to go to Jerusalem and there the Word of God told them that Bethlehem was their destination. When they obeyed the Word, the star reappeared and led them to the house where Jesus and Mary were waiting. You find this pattern given in Psalm 19. God reveals Himself in creation (vv. 1–6), the Scriptures (vv. 7–11), and then personally to the human heart (vv. 12–14). *The Magi did not stop until they came to Jesus and saw Him personally!*

There is a third truth to be learned: the Magi made worshiping Jesus the reason for their visit (Matt. 2:2, 8, 11). This should be the purpose of Christmas for all of God's people, not just sharing gifts with each other but giving ourselves and our very best to Him. During the busy, demanding days of the season, we must not forget to take time to worship the Lord and thank Him for coming to save us.

In this ancient scene, there is also a warning: people can know all the facts about the birth of Christ and not know Jesus personally. Herod and the Jewish religious leaders knew where Jesus was, but they did not go to see Him. St. Augustine wrote, "They [the Jewish religious leaders] were like milestones: they pointed out something to travelers, but themselves remained stolid and motionless." Those who truly seek Jesus will find Him (Isa. 55:6–7) and be found by Him (Luke 19:10).

The Savior of the world was just a few miles away from Jerusalem, yet the Jewish leaders made no move to see Him. The Queen of Sheba was a Gentile and yet she traveled a great distance to learn wisdom from Solomon, and the Magi traveled a long way to worship the newborn King. In the judgment they will be witnesses against the religious people who knew the facts but ignored Him who is the truth (John 14:6; Matt. 12:42). What a tragedy it would be to "celebrate" Christmas and yet reject the Christ of Christmas!

❦ See: Gifts, Herod the Great, Joy, Questions, Star

189

WORD

"In the beginning was the Word, and the Word was with God, and the Word was God" (John 1:1). This is the way the apostle John introduces the Son of God, the Lord Jesus, to the readers of his Gospel. This may seem a strange way to begin the story of Jesus, but the Greeks to whom John was writing were philosophical, interested in the unseen realities behind the visible universe. To the Greek thinkers, the Word (or Logos) was a technical term for the Mind or Reason that guided the universe. "Word" was one of the ways they thought of God.

The Hebrew people also used the term *word* as a synonym for God in His activity. God's "word" was His self-expression, found in the law (Deut. 30:11–14) and in His wisdom (personified in Proverbs 8). Both Jews and Gentiles understood that John was referring to God by his use of "Word."

John made several claims for "the Word" in the opening words of his Gospel. He stated that the Word is God (1:1) and that the Word is "with God" (vv. 1–2). The Word is the source of creation (v. 3) and also provides spiritual life and light (v. 4). John's greatest claim is that "the Word became flesh" (v. 14). This is the doctrine of the incarnation, that God the Son permanently took to Himself a human nature and body and entered the human world of time and space.

Consider what the experience of incarnation meant to our Lord Jesus Christ. The words of Philippians 2:5–11 are our window to understanding:

Your attitude should be the same as that of Christ Jesus:

> Who, being in very nature God,
> did not consider equality with God something to
> be grasped,
> but made himself nothing,
> taking the very nature of a servant,
> being made in human likeness.
> And being found in appearance as a man,

he humbled himself
and became obedient to death—
even death on a cross!
Therefore God exalted him to the highest place
and gave him the name that is above every name,
that at the name of Jesus every knee should bow,
in heaven and on earth and under the earth,
and every tongue confess that Jesus Christ is Lord,
to the glory of God the Father.

When the Son of God took on flesh, the Creator became a creature. The God who spoke the universe into existence became a two-celled person (creature) in the womb of Mary. The incarnation also meant the Sovereign became a servant. The Son of God whose every word was obeyed instantly in heaven had come to earth to obey the Father and fulfill the divine plan of salvation.

Jesus is named in Scripture as the Prince of Life, the Prince of Peace, and the Prince of Glory. Princes are royal, and royalty is rich. In His incarnation, the Prince became a pauper. Jesus "made himself nothing" (emptied Himself) in becoming human, surrendering the independent exercise of His divine attributes. He did not cease to be God but He submitted the use of His divine prerogatives to the Father's will. Jesus exchanged glory for poverty.

In His incarnation, the Shepherd became the sacrifice. Shepherd is one of the titles for God in the Old Testament (Gen. 49:24) and Jesus is the Good Shepherd in the New Testament (John 10:11, 14). By embracing "death on a cross," the Good Shepherd became "the Lamb of God, who takes away the sin of the world" (1:29). So there was a significant "stooping down" as the Word became flesh.

Let's transition from thinking of *Word* as a theological term to thinking of it in everyday terms: as a tool of communication. Words are dynamic—they inform us, captivate us with a story, or motivate us to act. We use words to express our thoughts and feelings, and to explain and guide our decisions. Words are the building blocks of communication. Jesus is God's final and fullest communication to us. In Jesus, God is speaking just the right Word to us.

The Word That Defines

Jesus is the Word that defines. Jesus defines reality: there is a God, God is our Creator, and Jesus Himself is God come to save us. Jesus defines the human condition: we are dead and in need of life (John 1:4). We are in the dark, needing light (v. 5). There is a battle raging between light and darkness, and darkness will not win (v. 5). Jesus also defines God's nature: God is personal and relational and He acts to save sinners. The Word is the Second Person of the Godhead, so Jesus helps us understand the doctrine of the Trinity: there is one God in three eternal, equal Persons.

The Word That Introduces

Jesus is also the Word that introduces. Jesus came to earth to invite us into a relationship with God (vv. 10–12). When we make an introduction, we use words to name each person and to give information that will initiate conversation. "Noah, I'd like to introduce you to Seth. Seth is an avid turkey hunter like you and he works in corporate finance. Seth, Noah works at our local bank and he lives on a farm with some prime turkey habitat." Now those two can begin talking to each other.

Jesus came to the world that He created, but few recognized Him when He showed up (v. 10). Those who should have known Him, rejected Him (v. 11). The film *It's a Wonderful Life* portrays this experience when George Bailey is granted his wish to have never been born. He returns to his hometown of Bedford Falls only to discover it has been renamed Pottersville. He can name the town's citizens, but none of them recognize him. "Don't you know me?" draws a negative response every time, and it's heartbreaking.

Those who receive Jesus, or believe on His name (v. 12), begin a relationship in which God is Father and they are God's children. Only Jesus can make this introduction, because "no one comes to the Father but through Me" (14:6 NASB). To know God as Father, we have to meet Him on His terms, not ours. God is holy; therefore sin must be punished. Jesus was punished for our sins on the cross. Those who come to God must be righteous. When we believe in Jesus, His righteousness is credited to our account (Rom. 4:5), so God sees us through the righteousness of Christ. Salvation is a gift, and we have to receive it to be right with God.

The Word That Encourages

Jesus is also the Word that encourages. "The Word became flesh" (John 1:14) affirms that Jesus is both fully God and fully human, two natures coexisting in one divine, unique Person. Greek philosophy and Muslim theology both deny that God can or would become human. In those systems, matter is evil, so God would devalue Himself by becoming flesh.

But the Gospel of John tells us that the preexistent Son of God permanently took to Himself a human body and nature (vv. 14–15) and He remains the unique God-Man today. John affirms that the incarnation is a way to see the glory of the "only begotten of the Father" (KJV): the Son of God coming in humbleness, stooping to serve and sacrifice and triumph. When we see the incarnate Son of God, we also see grace and truth.

So it is good to be human—because Jesus is. He has experienced life as we do, and He understands what it means to live in this fallen world. Jesus knows about temptation, rejection, hostility, loneliness, sorrow, and pain. He also knows about love, family, joy, prayer, and friendship. That makes Him our great encourager. He, of course, did not sin. He helps us resist temptation and avoid sin. When we fail, He doesn't criticize us or desert us. He understands and encourages us to move forward. He transforms us by His grace and truth. With Jesus, life is worth living.

The Word That Explains

Jesus is the Word that explains. John tells us in 1:18 that Jesus is the one who has "explained" the Father to those who believe. In Greek the word *explained* is "exegeted." Exegesis is the science of revealing the substance and meaning of something—or Someone. The Son of God alone can give true expression to who God is. Jesus reveals God so that we can begin to comprehend (within our limitations) the person and work of God.

Jesus reveals what would be invisible without Him. "No one has seen God at any time; the only begotten God, who is in the bosom of the Father, He has explained Him" (v. 18 NASB). What is God like? When we look at Jesus, we see what God is like. The people of Israel knew God was their Father, but Jesus made the title of "heavenly Father" personal and intimate. God's power and wisdom can be seen in creation and in history, but it took Jesus for us to see that God is relational and approachable.

As the Word that explains, Jesus also solves some of life's mysteries. There is the mystery of existence: Why are we here? Jesus tells us we're here to know God, and be known by God, and enjoy and serve God. There is the mystery of evil: Why do innocent people suffer and why do evil persons seem to prosper? Jesus didn't give a final answer, but He showed how to defeat the devil and He conquered evil in His death on the cross. On the mystery of death, Jesus shines the light of resurrection: death is how we enter the "Father's house" (see John 14:2) and how we live even though we die (11:25).

As the Word that explains, Jesus also completes the human story. He provides insight into how the future unfolds: He builds His Church with and through us, He conquers the forces of evil, ultimately exercises a rule of peace from David's throne, and reigns in glory over the new heaven and earth. There is a happy ending for those who believe in and follow Jesus.

"The Word" is Jesus, God's Son in human form. The Word is the Creator and sustainer of the world. The Word is our Savior. The Word reveals God as our Father. The Word is powerful. We can resist Him and be in the dark or receive Him by believing and walk in the light.

In Jesus, God speaks just the Word that we need.

⟨ See: Firstborn, Immanuel, Incarnation, Jesus, Messiah, Virgin Birth

WORLD

Let's suppose you had to give a gift to each person in the world, a gift that was desperately needed and that would last forever. What would that gift be? Certainly not food, clothing, cars, games, appliances, or even money.

There is only one gift that qualifies, and it is described in a familiar verse, John 3:16—"For God so loved the world that he gave his one and only Son, that whoever believes in him shall not perish but have eternal life." Jesus is the only gift that is priceless, that everyone desperately needs, and that will last forever. Jesus is God's gift to the world.

The word *world* in this verse means "the world of people." Knowing what we do about ourselves and about the world of people around us, if you were God, *would you love this world?* Consider these descriptions of the world of people as found in the Bible.

> The LORD saw how great man's wickedness on the earth had become, and that every inclination of the thoughts of his heart was only evil all the time.
>
> *Genesis 6:5*

> Now the earth was corrupt in God's sight and was full of violence. God saw how corrupt the earth had become, for all the people on earth had corrupted their ways.
>
> *Genesis 6:11–12*

> The LORD looks down from heaven on the sons of men to see if there are any who understand, any who seek God. All

have turned aside, they have together become corrupt; there is no one who does good, not even one.

Psalm 14:2–3

For from within, out of men's hearts, come evil thoughts, sexual immorality, theft, murder, adultery, greed, malice, deceit, lewdness, envy, slander, arrogance and folly. All these evils come from inside and make a man "unclean."

the words of Jesus in Mark 7:21–23

The rest of mankind . . . still did not repent of the work of their hands; they did not stop worshiping demons, and idols of gold, silver, bronze, stone and wood—idols that cannot see or hear or walk. Nor did they repent of their murders, their magic arts, their sexual immorality or their thefts.

Revelation 9:20–21

If you were Jehovah God, is this the kind of world you would love? And to show your love, how would you go about changing it? The answer is that you would work gradually and patiently, changing one heart at a time. God called Abraham and Sarah, an elderly, childless couple, and from them built the nation of Israel. Through that nation He revealed Himself as the one true and living God, and through that nation He gave the world the Bible and the promise of the coming Redeemer. "But when the time had fully come, God sent his Son, born of a woman, born under law, to redeem those under law, that we might receive the full rights of sons" (Gal. 4:4–5).

Celebrating the birth of Jesus Christ should remind us that *we are greatly loved by God even though we do not deserve it!* When we were at our worst, God gave us His very best. The photographs of the Earth that have been taken from outer space show only a blue planet. They show nothing of the hearts, thoughts, and deeds of the people living on this planet. If they did, we would all be embarrassed.

When the Father sent His Son, what did He actually give to this undeserving world?

– W –

In Jesus Christ, God gives light to a dark world. "The people living in darkness have seen a great light; on those living in the land of the shadow of death a light has dawned" (Matt. 4:16, quoting Isa. 9:2). "The light shines in the darkness, but the darkness has not overcome it" (John 1:5 margin). Our world is covered by such moral and spiritual darkness that the minds of people cannot begin to grasp the awfulness of sin or the greatness of God's grace. "The god of this age [Satan] has blinded the minds of unbelievers, so that they cannot see the light of the gospel of the glory of Christ, who is the image of God" (2 Cor. 4:4).

In Jesus Christ, God offers forgiveness to a disobedient world. He could have sent Jesus to judge the world, but He sent Him to save the world. "The Father has sent his Son to be the Savior of the world" (1 John 4:14). Jesus is the Lamb of God who alone can take away the sins of the world (John 1:29). There is no statesman or politician, scientist or educator who can solve the deep problems in this world. The heart of every problem is the problem in the heart, and only Jesus Christ can forgive sins and change the human heart.

In Jesus Christ, God brings life to a dead world. Sin is not only darkness and disobedience; sin is death. "For the wages of sin is death, but the gift of God is eternal life in Christ Jesus our Lord" (Rom. 6:23). The difference between a believer and an unbeliever is not that one is better than the other but that the believer is alive in Christ and the unbeliever is dead in sin. "I tell you the truth," said Jesus, "whoever hears my word and believes him who sent me has eternal life and will not be condemned; he has crossed over from death to life" (John 5:24). "But because of his great love for us, God, who is rich in mercy, made us alive with Christ even when we were dead in transgressions" (Eph. 2:4).

In Jesus Christ, God demonstrates His love to a defiant world. "I am not a Christian believer," a flippant young man said to an evangelist. "What do you have to say to me?" The man replied, "I accuse you of being a rebel against the throne of the God who made you and keeps you alive!"

Nobody need ever question the love of God. "But God demonstrates his own love for us in this: While we were still sinners, Christ died for us" (Rom. 5:8). Sin is rebellion against God, and God has every right to destroy every rebel. Yet in His love, He sent His Son to die for our sins and thus bring about reconciliation with the God who made us and keeps us alive. "God . . . reconciled us to himself through Christ" (2 Cor. 5:18), and now His people say to the lost world, "We implore you on Christ's behalf: Be reconciled to God" (v. 20).

❦ See: **Glory, Grace, Light, Redemption**

XMAS

Since the mid-twentieth century, Christians have complained that the use of "Xmas" was a deliberate attempt to "take Christ out of Christmas." While there is no doubt that today's secular culture wants to remove "Christmas" and "Merry Christmas" from the English vocabulary, the original use of "Xmas" had no political or spiritual overtones.

That the first syllable of "Christmas" comes from the word *Christ* is indisputable. In Greek the name Christ is χριστός (*christos*). The first letter looks like the English letter X. Every vocation has its shorthand, and those in the church used the Greek letter chi (χ) to represent Christ in words that began with "Christ-." So "Xmas" is an honorable abbreviation for "Christmas."

Writing in the Middle Ages was expensive, especially the ink. So writers tried to conserve the precious fluid by using shorthand where possible. In letters, records, and books, χρι-στός was represented by chi. This carried into the English language. In the 1828 edition of Webster's Dictionary, the entry for "Xmas" reads, "As an abbreviation, X stands for Christ, as in

Xn. *Christian*; Xm. *Christmas*." Webster's 9th Edition (1983) still defines Xmas as "[X is symbol for Christ from the Greek letter chi (χ), initial of Christos Christ + mas (in Christmas)]: Christmas (dates from 1551)."

The X (or chi) is intended as an honorable shorthand way to say Christ, and Xmas is shorthand for Christmas (originally the service of worship centered on the birth of Jesus Christ, but eventually referring to the season as well).

The truth about the origin of "Xmas" will probably not cure the misbelief that "Xmas" is an attempt to remove Christ from Christmas. So if you're going to use "Xmas," do so with friends who understand the etymology of words and who will not doubt your reverence for Christ.

♪ See: Christmas, Epiphany, Yuletide

YULETIDE

The word *Yule* is from Old English (before the twelfth century), borrowed from Old Norse (*jul*), and means the feast of the nativity of Jesus Christ, or Christmas Day (December 25). Yuletide is the season from Christmas Eve until New Year's Day (or to Epiphany in the UK). *Christmastide* is a synonym, in use since 1626. A Yule log is a large log put on the hearth on Christmas Eve.

❦ See: Advent, Christmas, Epiphany, Xmas

ZECHARIAH

Alphabetically, in this book, Zechariah comes last; but chronologically, in Luke's Christmas birth narrative (Luke 1:5–25, 57–80), he is first. Dr. Luke begins with an old man and his wife and ends with the birth of the baby Jesus to a Jewish teenage mother. If you are looking for "generation gaps," you will not find them in the Christmas story. Luke definitely did not know the cliché "Christmas is for children."

There are at least thirty-one men in the Bible named Zechariah (meaning "Jehovah has remembered"), but this one is special. He was the father of John the Baptist, the man about whom Jesus said, "I tell you, among those born of women there is no one greater than John" (7:28). No matter how old you are, the more you meditate on Luke's account of Zechariah, the more encouragement it should give you.

Waiting for God's Answer

Scholars estimate that there were eighteen thousand priests serving in Jerusalem at the time Jesus was born, and there were not enough temple duties for all of them to serve at the same time. King David had divided the priests into twenty-four "courses," and Zechariah's course was the eighth (1 Chron. 24:1–19). Each division served two one-week periods a year and their ministries were chosen by lot. With that kind of a schedule, it would have been easy for Zechariah to "get caught in the system" and take his ministry for granted, but that did not happen. Zechariah was not like the careless priests described by Malachi in the first chapter of his book. Zechariah and his wife prayed faithfully at home, and he was prepared to pray at the temple.

What he was not prepared for was the sudden appearance of an angel and the answer to a lifelong prayer. Each day before the morning and evening sacrifices, the priests burned incense at the golden altar in the holy place (Exod. 30:1–8). The fragrant burning incense was a picture of devout prayer ascending to God from His worshiping people (Ps. 141:1–2). Zechariah and Elizabeth had been praying for a son all their married life, and now they were too old to have a family. But as Zechariah was ministering in the temple, the angel appeared to him and announced that they would have a son, and not just any son; their son would be the prophet that would go before the Messiah and prepare Israel for His arrival. This is the angel who would later say, "Nothing is impossible with God" (Luke 1:37).

Never stop praying, for God often sends the answer when we least expect it. Moses was routinely tending his father-in-law's sheep when God called him to lead Israel out of Egypt. Peter, Andrew, James, and John were managing their fishing business when Jesus called them to follow Him, and Matthew was collecting taxes for the Roman government. Paul and Silas were sharing in a worship service in Antioch when the Spirit called them to become missionaries. Sometimes the Lord likes to surprise us, so be alert!

Accepting God's Will

You would expect an old priest to be a man of great faith, but Zechariah must have forgotten about Abraham and Sarah and the miraculous birth of their son, Isaac, in their old age (Genesis 17; 21). His heart was happy at the good news but his voice was muted by his unbelief. He questioned God's word, so the Lord silenced Zechariah's words. The Bible pattern is "I believed, therefore I have spoken" (2 Cor. 4:13, quoted from Ps. 116:10); but Zechariah did not believe, so temporarily he lost the power to speak.

Sometimes accepting the will of God has a dark side to it, as with the sword in Mary's soul (Luke 2:34–35) or the thorn in Paul's flesh (2 Cor. 12:1–10). We must say with Jesus in the garden, "Father, if you are willing, take this cup from me; yet not my will, but yours be done" (Luke 22:42). The will of God is the expression of the love of God for us and we have nothing to fear. The angel's first words to Zechariah are good words for us: "Do not be afraid" (1:13).

Being Silent

During Elizabeth's nine months of pregnancy, Zechariah could neither speak nor hear (Luke 1:59–64). He and Elizabeth must have communicated with signs and used the writing tablet, but think of how inconvenient that must have been. But Zechariah could still meditate on God's Word and pray silently with his godly wife.

Perhaps Zechariah's beautiful song of praise (vv. 68–79) was the fruit of those long months of silence and meditation. Some believers today are so busy and talkative that a time of silence is a threat to them, especially in a worship service or a prayer meeting. They seem to ignore verses like Psalm 4:4—"Search your hearts and be silent"—or Psalm 46:10—"Be still, and know that I am God." Solomon reminds us that there is "a time to be silent and a time to speak" (Eccles. 3:7), and wise is the believer who knows what time it is.

"God is the friend of silence," said Mother Teresa. "Trees, flowers, grass grow in silence." So do God's children.

Expressing Joys

First, the meditative silence, then the song of praise (Luke 1:68–79). Zechariah did not think of himself but of the Lord and His people. He praised God for the salvation that Mary's Son would accomplish. Because of His sacrifice on the cross, He would release us from bondage (v. 68), defeat our enemies (vv. 69, 71, 74), cancel the debt of our sin (vv. 76–77), and usher in the dawning of a new day (vv. 78–79). Zechariah and Elizabeth may never have seen Jesus as an adult, but they rejoiced at what He would do for the sinful world.

It is unfortunate that many of the songs used during the Christmas season are not biblical, and some of them are just plain juvenile. Let's not criticize Zechariah because of his un-belief. Let's give thanks to God that this elderly man used his months of silence for the kind of meditation and prayer that produced the magnificent song (the Benedictus) recorded in Luke's Gospel.

We are silent that we might listen to God. Then we speak and praise Him that we might glorify God. Blessed are the balanced!

𝄞 See: Elizabeth, Faith, John the Baptist, Joy, Songs

Between them, Warren and David Wiersbe have pastored seven churches, providing a rich background of Advent and Christmas traditions. Their personal and pastoral experiences prompted *C Is for Christmas*. This is the father-son team's fifth book together.

Warren W. Wiersbe is a pastor, author, and editor of more than 150 books, including *50 People Every Christian Should Know*, *On Earth as It Is in Heaven*, and *On Being a Servant of God*. He lives in Nebraska.

David W. Wiersbe has been a pastor for over thirty years. He is the author of *The Dynamics of Pastoral Care* and *Gone but Not Lost*, as well as coauthor of five books with his father, and lives in Minnesota.

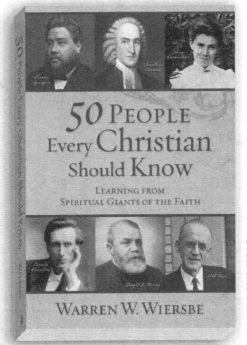

Made in the USA
Middletown, DE
20 October 2015